Advance praise for
The 60 Seconds Fix

I really enjoyed this book, and while the scientific evidence was compelling, the skeptic in me wasn't ready to accept a "60 seconds fix." Then, I tried it for myself, and it worked! Just like Melrose reports in her stories, I now go back to sleep effortlessly.

~ Krishna Pendyala
Director of the Mindful Nation Foundation
Author of *Beyond the Pig and the Ape: Realizing Success and True Happiness*

Upset is upset and happy is happy for a reason—human beings are hard-wired for happiness! Dr. Melrose provides the critical path for achieving optimal human functioning with 60 Seconds. Prepare to love its simplicity!

~ Marlaine "Mama Marlaine" Cover, MPA
Creator of The Life Skills Report
Author of *Kissing the Mirror: Raising Humanity in the Twenty-First Century*

If you are like me, you want to be more productive, and no matter how well you've learned how to do it, there always seems to be another idea that will end up taking more time than it saves. Not with *The 60 Seconds Fix*! Melrose cuts out the hours of study and training and presents ideas that cut to the chase. A fun, refreshing way to rid yourself of unwanted habits and become as productive as you want to be.

~ Warren Whitlock
Business Growth Advisor
Bestselling author of *Twitter Revolution: How Social Media and Mobile Marketing is Changing the Way We Do Business and Market Online* and *Profitable Social Media - Business Results Without Playing Games*

I love this book! As a typically over-scheduled businesswoman in the corporate world, I have wanted a quick easy way to calm my nerves and find my focus before going into meetings, phone calls, and negotiations. *The 60 Seconds Fix* has given me a complete toolkit that works every time! If you want to know how to stay on top of your game, no matter what kind of pressure you're under, get busy reading this book.
~ Michelle Balog
Real Estate Agent
Author of *SKIRT Working: How to Network Using SKIRT*

In today's fast-paced world, we could all use a simpler, more time-efficient way of solving problems and a calm, more clearheaded way to deal with challenges. Whether it is better focus on the job, more peace in relationships, or greater power over ourselves, Dr. Reggie teaches us how to manage our emotions, reactions, and impulses to get more of what we want out of life with greater ease.
~ Dr. Beth L. Halbert
America's Teenologist
Author of *Embracing Defiance: Helping Your Child Express Their Unique Voice While Keeping Your Sanity*

The 60 Seconds Fix reminds us of how powerful our mind is. Through self-regulation, visualization, and proper breathing, one can change one's unhealthy attitude in just one minute. "Self" is the key concept here—by redirecting her readers from the outside foundations of happiness to the internal sources of inspiration needed for mental well-being, Dr. Regalena Melrose effectively empowers us all.

~ Janusz Wrobel
Author of *Contact: The Tale of Human Longing for Fulfilling Communication* and *Language and Schizophrenia*

Dr. Regalena Melrose has done it again! This laugh-out-loud explanation of how self-regulation makes one's life not only better and manageable, but also fulfilling and joyful, captures the vibrant character and message of Dr. Melrose. Her effervescent personality reaches into the heart and mind of the reader from the first page and takes us through a journey of self-discovery, humor, and hope. Combining her expertise of neuroscience with her unique way of making the reader feel completely accepted and understood makes this book a MUST-READ for any and all who want to REALLY LIVE their lives.

~ Virginia Donnell, M.A.
School Psychologist

Dr. Melrose has done it—she's brought the benefits of meditation and mindfulness to those of us who don't have time for yoga or don't buy into frou-frou spiritual groups, yet still want a healthier way of dealing with stress than the next margarita, cigarette, or outburst. She seamlessly weaves humor, science, and stories together in this must-read book for anyone who lives life on the go, stressed out, crashed out, or overwhelmed with the hectic pace of modern life (and isn't that most of us?). *The 60 Seconds Fix* is not only a serious game-changer, but fun to read, down-to-earth, not stuffy with "shoulds" but encouraging with "coulds." Reading this book, and then having the experience of 60 Seconds regularly, shows us how we can easily feel better, and then do better, more often, without any external pacifiers. Dr. Melrose gets us in touch with our own natural calm in such an accessible yet profound way, making 60 Seconds the cheapest, healthiest "drug" on the market! Simple. Powerful!

   ~ Nancy Woo
     Writer and Editor

The 60 Seconds Fix is practical, down-to-earth, easy to understand, doable and life-changing. Dr. Melrose gives us the tools to achieve the best and most efficient use of our brains. A must-read for anyone who wants to be happy, effective, and creative in these noisy, distracting, and demanding times!

   ~ Michael Houlihan
     Creator of Barefoot Wine, America's #1 wine brand
     New York Times bestselling author of *The Barefoot Spirit*

The
60 Seconds
Fix:

*The Brain-Changing Toolkit
That Stops Unwanted Habits
and Starts Surprising Joy*

Regalena Melrose, Ph.D.

ISBN-13: 978-0615888682
ISBN-10: 0615888682

Printed in the United States of America

The 60 Seconds Fix:
The Brain-Changing Toolkit That Stops Unwanted
Habits and Starts Surprising Joy

Published by:
60 Seconds Press
3519 E Second St,
Long Beach, CA

For my clients

Table of Contents

Acknowledgments

This book was possible only because of learning from, and growing with, Stephen Sova. Thank you, my friend.

Angela, James, and Wellington: thank you for telling me, simply, "It's time," and for seeing bumper stickers, mugs, and t-shirts! ☺ I started writing this book because of you.

Kekor, your pure love has kept me on this path with clarity. Thank you.

Nancy and Ginger: you are editors extraordinaire and sisters who seriously rock!

To all the schools that happily committed to bringing 60 Seconds and Brain Charge to life: a very special note of tremendous appreciation. I hope you will always take pride in what you have accomplished with yourselves and the students in your care. I want to make special mention of some of you here: Susan, Lisa, Judy, Charlie, Dave, Shaun, Beth, Jad, Christian, Tya, Alex, Ruth, Barbara, Despina, and Lew. There are so many more of you. Forgive me for not knowing all of you personally, and for not knowing more directly how beautifully you are carrying on this work.

To all the others who have never stopped believing in me, and my mission. You have stood beside me holding the vision. Please know how that has kept me going even when the only thing I wanted to do was give up. To my dear clients, my irreplaceable best friends, every one of you, my spiritual community, and my family. I am grateful beyond measure.

Preface

After years of giving the talk I do on *how* to feel good now, I am thrilled to report that the proverbial mountain has moved! People are "getting it!" The number of us who believe we can be in a naturally good feeling state more often is growing. We are becoming more determined than ever to learn what we need to do to get more instantaneous relief from our stressful lives without resorting to unhealthy habits. Thanks to some awesome neuroscience, we have finally figured out how to have greater ease and bigger joy for longer than a beer buzz! Can you believe it?! I know...It's crazy. ☺ Discovering that "miracle" has changed my life.

I used to feel frustrated by the "mountain"—the audiences that wouldn't budge no matter what I did to inspire. I was so excited about discovering "the miracle," I wanted to show everyone how they could experience it too. In front of one audience after another, even now, I do slapstick, handstands, and cartwheels. Whatever it's going to take to move the mountain, I'm happy to do it! By showing them how to give themselves the good feeling while we're together, I convince most of the audience much of the time. Later, however, I sometimes learn that since hearing me speak and feeling such relief and hope, in their daily lives, they're not "finding the time." No matter how excited they get about my cartwheels in the moment, on their own, they aren't doing what it takes to get that feeling again. ☹

It's not easy to find time. We juggle so much—and very well, by the way—but let's face it, we often look like a circus act on steroids, not to mention how we feel. The kind of multi-tasking we do is unbelievable! Yet surprisingly, as much as I thought it was the errands and the kids and our careers making it impossible to find time to take care of ourselves, I realized that what was wastefully burning up our precious time and energy was worrying. Worrying and complaining; gossiping and venting; judging and labeling; and, my personal favorite: criticizing. We spend an *inordinate* amount of time criticizing ourselves worst of all!

Do you remember Diane Weist's character in Woody Allen's *Bullets Over Broadway*? In my favorite scene she urges her lover to stop. "Don't speak," she says dramatically as she covers his mouth, "Don't speak," she says emphatically, each time more so than the last. I have come to learn from the changes I've made in my own life that when I can hear Diane's voice and I can just stop speaking, I find a lot of time.

Knowing to just stop talking helps. Yet even when we tell ourselves to stop, even when we clearly see that not being able to contain our ramblings is wasting time or making things worse, we can't stop! Without the tools to soothe the dis-*ease* inside of us (NOT disease!) that causes the verbal diarrhea, it's impossible. We're off and running with our reaction to a situation, rather than a thoughtful response. Or, even when we have something great to say, sometimes the person on the other end simply can't hear us in the moment.

Words. They sure can be miserable sometimes. The ones on the inside are thoughts that peck at our brain, rile up our nervous system, and ready us for some kind of battle that's mostly between our ears, even if we've picked a target outside ourselves. We can free ourselves from these words though, and doing so is surprisingly easy and fun! The question is, "Do we want to? Do we really *want* to stop the old stories in our brain and just feel good, for more than the fleeting moments of happiness from a bottle?" I'm talking about healthy, long-term, steady-Eddy joy that just keeps bubbling up in the simplest of moments without any aid from pharmaceuticals at all. Say what!? I'm serious! It's possible!

I know this sounds far-fetched in a world moving faster than ever. We're so stressed we believe we have some kind of disorder. We must! We have all the signs and symptoms listed in the commercials, right? And there's a pill for that so it can't be that bad...

Hmmmm...

Woody Allen was on to something in another of his films, *Vicki Christina Barcelona*, when Patricia Clarkson's character is convinced she is "trapped" in an unhappy marriage. She explains quite plainly that she is waiting for a magical solution. Boy, can I relate to that! I think we've been hoping the pills would be that magical solution. And who can blame us? A little "pixie dust" to free us from the prison of our discontent sounds good to me. I tried pixie dust for a while—in its many varieties actually: vodka pixie dust; antidepressant pixie dust; my list goes on. All the while I wondered, because the "magic" was sadly temporary, *Which pixie dust is it going to take? There has to be at least one that will work over the long haul, at least one that won't have side effects that numb my brain, disguise my personality, or ruin my life.*

I finally got to that place we've all experienced at one time or another—the "sick and tired of feeling sick and tired" place. Paraphrasing Anais Nin, there came a day when the pain of staying the same outweighed the pain of change. I realized I was going to have to figure out for myself what the true magic was going to be. I started listening more – to my body and my life. I read, I experienced, I discovered, and wouldn't you know it? I ended up with a solution that felt pretty magical. Over the course of 15 years, I integrated information and tools until everything organically morphed together to become a single, fun, easy, simple way of feeling good. I'm talking about feeling good without having to spend money I don't have or eat food I can't fit in my stomach. I no longer need to rely on *anything* outside of my own internal resources to get relief.

This miracle of a discovery is something I call "60 Seconds" because it only takes 60 seconds to begin to feel its effects. Everyone in my life—audience members, colleagues, clients, students, family, and friends—now experience instantaneous relief from using the toolkit in their daily life. I spent years observing and documenting its effects, *as I remained a skeptic.* It was too simple and easy to do. Surely, the promising results would turn out to be a fluke. They would wear off and prove over time to be as disappointing as the many other interventions we've all tried before. That is not what happened. With a team of 60 Seconds benefactors and believers, I have collected beautiful data and observed amazing results. Every age group, from two to 82, that has utilized these **five little tools in one little minute,** no matter what the presenting problem seems to be, has experienced its positive effects: higher achievement, greater focus, less anxiety, more calm, less reactivity, better concentration, and more sleep! The power of 60 Seconds is real!

Gently and with ease, I see how 60 Seconds is breaking us free from the only prison that really exists – the confines of our own brain-body. That's a strange term when we hear it the first time, but the "brain-body" is what neuroscientists refer to as the integrated whole of our brain and body working together, which they always do. The brain and body influence each other, at all times, making us feel either better or worse. Inside our brain and throughout our body, numerous processes are at work: psychological, physiological, biological, and biochemical. These processes can keep us from what we really want when we don't know how to regulate them. I know we want lifelong feelings of relief, joy, passion, connection, balance, and peace. We want peace on the job, in our family, and on our planet, if only we could stop reacting to the daily challenges we face. In order to have what we want, in order to have peace outside of us, we must know how to have it on the inside. That comes from knowing *how* to calm the brain-body in seconds.

Remember in the film, *Silver Linings Playbook* (*when do I have time to see all these movies?* I find myself wondering...), Bradley Cooper's character, Pat, goes to see his psychiatrist, repeatedly, and the psychiatrist, like a broken record, says to him, "Find your tools, Pat. Use your tools." For those of you who didn't see the movie, the psychiatrist gives Pat this instruction over and over again and *not once* teaches him a single tool! All he did, each time Pat made a visit, was instruct: "Find your tools, Pat. Use your tools." I wanted to scream through the screen, "Isn't that what Pat's paying *you* for?!" Who are these doctors getting paid to tell us the obvious? "No kidding, I need some tools! Do you think I landed here with YOU because I have tools?! *Teach them to me!*"

Happy hour is not a tool, by the way. Discovering that truth was one of the biggest bummers of my life. Happy hour is one of those rare advertisements that's actually true. I was happy for the hour. So happy, I extended my stay and started calling it "happy hours." I had my Monday friend for "happy hours," and my Tuesday friend for "happy hours." You get the picture. I was happy...and then not so much.

The kind of feeling good I talk about now, the kind of freedom I want us all living in now, is not temporary. It's not of the variety, *I'll just discreetly pop this little pill in my mouth; no one will even notice and everything will be fine.* I'm talking about freedom from all the meds—Xanax, sleeping pills, antidepressants – most of what doctors today are prescribing. If it's working for you—if you're getting all the benefits without the side effects—if your life is being enhanced and not compromised as a result, then by all means, please keep doing what is helping you feel good. I'm not here to rain on anyone's parade. However, if, like me, what you're currently using to feel better, a substance, a behavior, an activity, a habit, or a thought pattern, is turning against you, costing you more than its dividends, I want you to know there's another way. Not a dry, dull or boring way. That just wouldn't be prudent!

The path I am walking now is nowhere near the path of Mother Theresa, believe me, but it's also nowhere near my days of some pretty serious misery. I knew no way out of that misery no matter how many therapy sessions I had, seminars I went to, or self-help books I read. The path I walk now is much easier and more fun than any of that. It started after I asked myself some important questions. I'll ask them of you now:

Do you want more time for the things you are passionate about, the things you've always wanted to find the time to do? Do you want to spend less time on your habits like gambling, shopping, video gaming, and watching television? Do you want more motivation to do things that really matter to you, like connecting with that friend, going for that walk, or writing that book? Do you want to use your drug of choice, like food, alcohol, or marijuana with greater moderation (or not at all) so you can feel more present and connected to yourself and your loved ones? How about staying calmer with your kids rather than overreacting or yelling when you don't really need to? Do you want to rise to the top of your game and have greater success with your career? What about break free of diagnoses, labels, old stories, and self-criticisms that keep you in an incessant cycle of wanting to make a change, starting to make a change, yet falling right back into the same old way of doing things?

If you answered yes to any of these questions, I have such good news. It comes from a traditionally stuffy place—the ivory tower of science. However, unlike any scientific discovery that has ever been revealed before, current neuroscience is blazing a new—REALLY NEW—path for the possibility of all our desires without having to follow any past or current trends in health. Twelve-step programs, for example, yoga, mindfulness, and other types of meditation have all benefitted many and continue to do so. No question. For others of us, however, it is a relief to know, **there is a simpler, less time-consuming way to develop moderation, balance, focus, and vigor.** 60 Seconds helps us eliminate the shame of our imperfection; it helps give us the power that is rightfully ours; and it regulates our emotions whether we're in the middle of a confrontation or we're asleep. And guess what? No matter what route we are already taking towards relief, whether that is yoga, talk therapy, medication, or a 12-step program, 60 Seconds is the catalyst that can propel our progress to the point that we may no longer need whatever else we're doing. That's exactly what happened to me and what continues to happen for so many of my clients.

Insert cartwheel. (Now visualize this: short petite brunette with long hair and dark eyes doing a cartwheel while exuding a huge smile from her face.) This is the spot in my talk when I have to be extra convincing by doing some sort of pony trick. When I do, everyone laughs, and it opens us all up just a little bit more to the newness. Since you can't see any of my actual twirls and spins, please do your part in visualizing the moment. ☺

Neuroscientific findings have exquisitely simplified our approaches to wellbeing. That's why I'm so excited! Our desires are more easily achieved when we possess within us what neuroscientists call self-regulation. Let's ponder that word. *Self*-regulation. This is a natural, internal, automatic capacity to balance our emotional states. With self-regulation, we need nothing external to us, only what is on the inside, in order to have more self-control, self-discipline, self-initiation, self-containment, and self-actualization. Everything we want, and I do mean everything, whether that's success or the happiness success brings, requires and begins with this capacity. The natural ebb and flow of the nervous system when it is internally balanced between tension and relief, in just the right amount, in just the right way, means we can be less emotionally reactive and more thoughtfully responsive. *Pretty cool*, is what I'm thinkin'.

What it takes to self-initiate, persist, feel motivated, be engaged, interested, curious, passionate, focused, determined, and strong is found *within* us. It comes when our nervous system is in its "flow," NOT stuck on either high or low. In fact, that's what business leaders call it: "The Flow." Professional athletes call it "The Zone." It's the perfect amount of excitement that keeps us engaged in life without being overwhelmed by it. What we've learned from the neuroscience, and even more clearly from our own experience, is that self-regulation and all the moderation it brings is not something we can talk ourselves into. No matter how strong our will, how great our desire, how detailed our plan of execution, without self-regulation the changes we want to make, the changes *we begin to make* cannot be sustained. Sustenance comes from an internal automatic ebb and flow that keeps us in The Zone.

Before MRIs were able to disprove our now-dated theories and notions of human behavior, the old way of thinking had us believe that if we didn't develop self-regulation at an early age, it would be too late for us to develop it later. We would end up with diagnoses and labels that went hand in hand with medication, therapy, or a 12-step program. We have been taught to believe that something external to us would have to control our inability to regulate in order for us to know both balance and moderation. Please see the HUGE smile on my face as I write, "This simply isn't true!" This new era, the 21st century, with its sophisticated neuroscientific inquiry through the use of MRIs and other more elaborate measures, is giving us a trailblazing message for a different way that frees us from old ways of thinking and doing.

Self-regulation for moderation allows us to rise to the top of our game no matter what our role is on the planet. We finally know how to walk the walk. The era of talking the talk is over. Isn't that a relief? We don't have to fake it anymore! We're off the hook! We get to live more transparently. If you're tired of being a slave to your old thoughts, patterns, habits, and reactions, and you want an easy, fun way to be new, this is the book for you. I invite you to give it an experiential try – not a read through to ponder over – but a participatory, engaged-in-the-exercises-try. There is no way of creating change without experience. This is fact, according to the neuroscience. Our brain changes in response to experience, *not words!* So please, don't just read this book. Say yes to the *experience* of it. I implore you with a cartwheel. ☺

Introduction:
It's Too Simple, I Know!

If someone told you that the difference between living and dying required 60 seconds of your day, would you find 60 seconds? I have been asking that of my audiences across North America for years (albeit in different ways), and sometimes half the audience is completely convinced they don't have 60 seconds for themselves. *How would we ever fit that in?* We may find ourselves wondering. The suggestion alone that we find time, even for what in the long run will save our lives, and what in the short term will increase the quality of life immeasurably, alarms us. "We can't afford to take the time to do *that*," we say. "That would be something I do for my*self*," as though taking care of ourselves is selfish. This old way of thinking keeps us from being healthy! Consider current stats: a *whopping* 50% of our child and adolescent population meet criteria for one disorder or another![1] Can you believe that?! I've got to tell you, when I look around sometimes, including *in the mirror,* I see who kids have for parents these days, and I can't be surprised. We're chickens with our heads cut off!

I juggle family with work, too, as many of us do. I get it. Most days, I live by the clock *to the minute!* I recently had a friend meet me at my son Jules' school where I was dropping him off before heading to the airport. I told my friend that if she wanted to drive me, I needed her at the school to pick me up at 8:25 if I was going to make the plane. When she didn't get to the school until, GOD FORBID - 8:29 - *how DARE she* - I can tell you those four minutes felt like the most stressful minutes of my life! *Not another opportunity to practice what I preach, darnit?! Is that what this is?* Have you ever noticed that? We put something out there and then we're tested to "walk the walk." The old me would not have liked that one bit, but now I love every chance I get to put my tools to the test. They work!

I remember a few years back, when Jules was almost four, his teacher called to talk about his aggressive behavior. He was hitting little girls! ☹ I was mortified. I was working at the time as a consultant to educators on how to reduce anger and aggression in schools while at home I was raising the next Mike Tyson. If I didn't have my tools, I tell you...my body surged in those moments the school called, with every chemical, hormone, and neurotransmitter driving me to want to murder! But you know what? Not one person ended up dead. Thank you 60 Seconds. ☺

You would think after using my tools with such great results for as long as I have, I would stop being so shocked every time they work, but I am. Every time I see my clients, students, friends, and colleagues get well quickly from the use of 60 Seconds, I am flabbergasted. It's too simple! Yet, my son and I are both doing better than ever. We haven't had a call from the school since he learned 60 Seconds, and when my friend arrived at the school to drive me to the airport, though my body had its moment of feeling like I could kill her, I remained self-contained, with ease, and our friendship prevailed. Victory once again.

Moments of extreme stress on the body challenge our relationships all the time. In fact, stress affects us even when it's not extreme. Sometimes it's more moderate, but ever present. That's when it insidiously accumulates in the brain-body over time without our conscious awareness. (Remember from the preface, the term brain-body refers to the integrated whole of our brain and body working together, which they always do. One always affects the other.) Our connections with others can easily become strained when we don't know how to manage the effects of stress on our own. We snap at the people we love, or worse. We distance ourselves from those we are closest to, from those upon whom we depend, and sometimes, from those who depend upon us. When experiencing stress without the capacity to regulate it, we inevitably withhold from our own children what they *desperately* need for healthy development and wellbeing throughout their lives (parents, please see the appendix for more).

In our stressful moments, I know it seems there is no way, no time, and no how to calm that agitated response. It feels automatic, instinctual and beyond our control. But it doesn't have to stay that way. What if I told you that even under the most stressful of circumstances you could have an entirely different experience of yourself, your loved ones, your coworkers and your environment, with only 60 seconds a day? If I had a whole lot of recent neuroscience to back up my claim, would that be even more convincing? Would that be convincing enough to get you to try for at least 21 days in a row a 60-second toolkit I have created for people just like you? I really hope so because the reason I am writing this book is so you'll give this miracle discovery a try. Time for joy, don't you think?

Here's my challenge to you: Read this book, learn 60 Seconds, practice it each day for at least 21 days, and observe, even document if you will, the difference you experience in your body, in your mind, and in your life. I promise to be both entertaining and convincing with hard science, personal stories, and anecdotal evidence from the work I do with many: men and women just like you and me; students of every age and grade level; clients at every stage of life with every kind of diagnosis you've ever heard; parents at every economic level, rich, poor, and in between; and finally, educators all over North America who have been implementing 60 Seconds in their classrooms, who continue to report the dramatic difference it is having in every facet of their lives, both personal and professional.

60 Seconds is a toolkit you can return to at any time. I recommend you bookmark this page, or copy and print it to post somewhere so you can refer to it every day:

1. Sitting in a chair, the couch, your car, or under a tree (it doesn't really matter where), uncross your legs or feet, and **feel your feet flat on the ground**. If, in the moment, you are unable to sit down, simply feel your feet flat on the ground if you are standing, or flat on the bed, by bending your knees up if you are lying down.

2. If you are able to sit or lie down, **take in the support of what you are sitting or lying in**. Lean into the back of the chair (for example). Feel your bottom sinking into the cushion of the couch (for another example), with your back resting in the cushions behind you or beneath you.

3. **Breathe in through your nose**, simply noticing that you are breathing, and with each breath – (remember, in through your nose) - fill your belly with air. Breathe out through your nose or mouth, whichever feels most comfortable.

4. **Visualize a soothing nature scene**, such as the beach, a meadow or flowing stream; or imagine some other safe and beautiful place that is just for you. You can do this with your eyes open or closed, whichever feels most comfortable to you.

5. **Now *most* importantly, notice what is happening inside your body** as you utilize

these first four of the five tools: *grounding* your feet; taking in *support*; *breathing* in through your nose, filling your belly with air; and *visualizing* a safe, beautiful place.

- As you utilize the fifth tool, *noticing* what is happening inside, focus only on the *pleasant* physical sensations you are having. Consider some of the words that would describe these sensations: warm, flowing, calm, vibrating, tingling, spacious, open, expanded, decreasing tension or tightness, slowing down, getting heavy, becoming clear-minded, focused, stabilized, solid, balanced, or connected.

- If thoughts or unpleasant sensations enter into your awareness, simply go back to the beginning of 60 Seconds and do the steps again. The more you notice *pleasant* sensations, the less you will focus on negative or distracting thoughts (more on all this later).

The following seven chapters will explain why these five tools (grounding, support, breath, visualization, and noticing) are so essential to living the quality of life we want without sacrificing too much time. Throughout the chapters, I will explain why the fifth step of *noticing* is the key to having a healthier, more joyful life as quickly as possible. In fact, at the end of each chapter will be what I call, "Playtime." This will be an opportunity to practice *noticing* the effect of each tool introduced in each chapter. Throughout Playtime, my words will lead you through an exercise that will help you to feel relief, comfort, and calm. If, however, while reading this book, during Playtime or at any other time, you notice uncomfortable feelings or sensations, please put the book down and use whichever of the tools you have learned so far to notice the resources you have within you and around you to relieve the discomfort. This book is meant to address what is really going on in our lives, and some of it may be painful! However, the book is also meant to address our lives in a way that empowers us with tools that help. Read slowly. Use Playtime to learn how to feel good in spite of what is challenging.

60 Seconds has the power to give us what it takes to transcend the painful realities of life and be freer from the old thoughts, stories, beliefs, doubts, worries, fears, judgments, and criticisms that plague us. With 60 Seconds, I want us to have the experience of a more sincere and embodied peace so real, in fact, that we can't help but emanate joy to everyone with whom we come into contact. I want us to have the highest quality of life in the quickest amount of time; and perhaps most importantly, I want us to have lots of ease and fun in both getting there and being there.

Though I have witnessed this tool change the lives of hundreds of people over the years, if I wasn't living the difference myself, I would not be able to say with complete conviction that 60 Seconds is the tool that will help make peace and joy possible for you and your loved ones. You won't have it all tomorrow, and you'll never have it perfectly. We don't get to be perfect while having a human experience in physical form - at least I don't think we can (but I would love to be wrong)! What we do get is something that I think is better. We get to learn how to love and accept our imperfect selves, so our loved ones can do the same. In spite of a world moving faster with its ever increasing demands, we get to know *how* with 60 Seconds to slow ourselves down without judgment and criticism. We get to know *how* with 60 Seconds to have self-compassion that grows quickly into compassion for everyone around us.

Don't we love it when people tell us to "Settle down; simmer down; get it together," or my personal favorite, "Relax!" *Very relaxing indeed. Not!* If someone instructing you to "Calm down!" isn't working for you, please know that 60 Seconds is here to fill in the gap. This toolkit will give you "the how" that is starkly missing from well-intentioned people's painfully succinct advice. In fact, it is "the how" for pretty much any advice we've ever gotten. 60 Seconds and the self-regulation it creates is the foundation that makes *all* things possible because that's when we're at our best. It's neurochemical nirvana! It's our brain in its optimum state. And being able to get there 60 seconds at a time is MAGIC! Let's get started, shall we? ☺

1
Less Time Than
Opening A Bottle Of Wine

Have you ever driven home from work or school and then wondered how you got there? We do things automatically or on autopilot all the time. We operate outside of conscious awareness and when we do, we have what some people call an out-of-body experience. In fact, because of how quickly Western culture is now moving with global technology and fast-paced media, most of us live that way much of the time – completely detached from our own body, our greatest resource. For example, if I asked you in this moment whether or not your feet are on the ground, you would likely only begin to notice whether or not they are in order to answer the question, not because this is something of which you're consciously aware. ALL my clients, in fact, when they first start working with me, report that they often feel like they're floating through their daily lives, disconnected from the ground, from others, and from themselves. This is what it feels like to have high levels of stress hormones pumping through our blood. "Leaving" our body is a *natural* response to the unnatural pace of life today. Rushing around like the house is on fire doesn't feel good! Why would we want to be in our body to feel that?

Instead, we adaptively "go away" in any number of ways. To avoid feeling the uncomfortable physical sensations of our body under pressure, we do the opposite of what will actually make things better, especially in the long run. We keep as busy as we can with our to-do lists so there is little chance we will be still long enough to notice how uncomfortable we really are. Too many times, we find ourselves functioning in survival mode, like animals adapting in the wild. When we are required to sit down somewhere and interact with others in a more human fashion—as a social, cooperative being who can be still for more than a few minutes at a time—we may need to calm the uncomfortable physical sensations of stress that keep us in animal mode. That's when we might pour ourselves a drink, roll ourselves a joint, or eat a big piece of chocolate cake, and why not? It feels good!

Nectar from the gods is how I describe my first beer at age 13. It was euphoric to have found the answer to everything. I mean, I was only 13 and I had already found The Answer. Talk about advanced. The heavens opened up, the Red Sea parted, and I had my Ah-ha! Moment. All over a Bud Light. This is what happens when no one is talking about what's really going on—about how most of us, no matter what our age, don't have a clue how to cope with stress in a healthy way. Yet stress, we now know, is the silent culprit of all things going to pot. Like nearly every other child on earth, when I was a kid, I had to figure things out on my own. It was easy for people to say,

"Calm down. Relax." I remember thinking, *That sounds great,* while my insides were screaming something else a lot less polite: *I want to calm down, you asshole! What do you think, this is fun for me?* But with no one explicitly teaching me *how* to calm down and relax in a healthy way, and believe me no one was modeling it either, I had to pull an answer out of my you know what. We've all had to do that at one time or another, haven't we? Pull a really cold beer out of a really tight place? Just me?

The brain-body can get really creative in its attempts to feel better because it knows that when we thrive, or feel good, we survive. Some call this instinct. Others call it the ancient wisdom of the body. Either way, we are all hard-wired to figure out how to feel relief no matter where it comes from because that is what enables us to go on.

Our primitive brain is the part of the brain focused on our immediate relief. It does not have the sophistication to realize that much of what we do for instantaneous relief is harmful to us in the long run. When we learn to cope through times of stress by "letting off steam" with angry outbursts, for example, or by pouring ourselves into work, playing videogames, shopping, gambling, watching pornography or ingesting drugs, alcohol or food, we develop neural pathways in our brain for this to become our automatic go-to or habit. When this happens over time, many of us end up building a tolerance to the soothing effects of our pacifier of choice. Eventually, though it may take years, we are left needing more and more of the pacifier for less and less relief. The helpful effects fade as more of the ugly side effects take over and spoil our relationships and overall quality of life. When once we felt *in* control with our drug of choice readily at hand, we now feel *out* of control as it simply stops working for us in that same euphoric way. Now all it does is take the edge off for a short time, while in the long run, leaves us feeling guilty and ashamed that we resorted to it at all.

Many of us can relate to making a choice, consciously or otherwise, to pay the price for our self-medication, no matter how high. That's how important feeling good is to the brain-body; to experience the antidote to stress, we seek something, *anything*, that will help us feel relief, however briefly. I am convinced nonetheless that the only reason some of us self-medicate despite the costs is because we don't know how easy it can be to do it another way. 60 Seconds is a faster, healthier way to get the same or better results, *and* our use of 60 Seconds models for our children how they can soothe in a healthy way too.

We want the next generation to avoid the shame that comes from excessive escape in order to feel at ease. I'm sure of it. That's what happens over time for our children and for us: when we aren't taught healthy ways of regulating the stress and pressure of life, we start to feel out of control, like the stress and pressure are winning. We begin to recognize that escape gives us relief, and we begin to believe that we *need* that escape in order to feel better, whether we are escaping by drinking alcohol, like I did, screaming like a crazy person before isolating in a room and slamming the door, or playing a videogame. Even when we want to stop disconnecting from ourselves and others in these ways, the neurochemical surge or "fix" we get from this kind of extreme behavior is so intense so quickly, it's pretty hard to beat.

Luke

Luke's dream is to be a performer like Chris Brown. He sings. He dances. He is learning the keyboard. That is, when he is not busy playing Call of Duty and every other video game on the market today. Though he tries to keep it all in balance as a full-time student, he is more often overtaken by his overwhelm with the expectations, demands, deadlines, and examinations of school, and seeks refuge in the game. Without any other tool for self-regulation, he has developed a habit of self-soothing that he believes he cannot live without. He's right, in a way. Without replacing the gaming with something else that serves the same function just as well, it is likely that Luke's brain-body would not do well "white-knuckling it."

Luke sought talk therapy for a time for his inability to self-regulate the stress and big emotions that became an intrusive part of his life. His inability to self-regulate looked like depression, as it sometimes can. His "depression," however, was not what it appeared to be and talk therapy didn't work. In fact, talk therapy made things worse because Luke now knew better but still couldn't do better.

Recent neuroscience is helping us more clearly understand and differentiate between depression and apathy. An apathetic state, like the one Luke is in, is a physiological depletion in the brain-body brought on by stress, either chronic or extreme. *The New York Times* published an article on April 19, 2012, entitled "Post-Prozac Nation," in which several studies were compiled to bring about consideration of "depression" as a degenerative disease like Alzheimer's and Parkinson's.[2] In the article we learn that "in monkeys, chronic stress produces a syndrome with symptoms remarkably similar to some forms of human depression." Stressed monkeys lose interest in pleasure and become lethargic, for example, due to a loss of neural pathways in the hippocampus, the part of the brain that is functionally linked to other areas of the brain that regulate emotional states, such as the orbitofrontal cortex. More specifically, in stressed monkeys, neuronal birth or "neural genesis" in the hippocampus was low, causing the monkeys to exhibit the depressive-looking state of apathy. They were treated successfully by stimulating growth of neural pathways in the hippocampus, which leads to greater regulation.

The term "neural pathways" simply refers to brain cells in communication with one another, thereby forming an alliance to support a behavior. We, too, are capable of growing neural pathways back in the hippocampus, thereby strengthening the communication between the hippocampus and the orbitofrontal cortex where our capacity to self-regulate is mediated. When we engage in 60 Seconds, we produce a brain-body state that is antidotal to the experience of stress. The state of calm that is arrived at through 60 Seconds produces a neurochemical "soup" inside us that promotes the growth of essential neural pathways. In humans, neuronal birth is linked to states of calm that arise from what many now call "mindfulness." In numerous studies conducted over the past decade, mindfulness meditation has been found to keep the brain young, relieve anxiety and moodiness, lead to better decision making, reduce stress, increase the immune response, enhance attention, mood, and memory, change the structure of the brain, and reduce several medical conditions such as irritable bowel syndrome. [3] Mindfulness meditation in schools improves self-control, self-awareness, attention skills, and social skills. It increases positive emotions, as well as decreases anxiety, blood pressure, and aggression.[4]

What I have witnessed over the past decade in myself and countless others is that 60 Seconds is the quickest, most convenient way to reach this state of "mindfulness" and benefit from all of its well-researched effects. It is a standing, sitting, walking, talking, washing-yourself-in-the-shower, driving, or waiting-in-line toolkit, NOT a meditation that requires sitting down quietly in a peaceful place. Who can find time for *that?!* No matter where we are or what we're doing, the first second we begin noticing our feet solidly planted on the ground is the second we begin building neural pathways out of self-medication and into self-regulation, presence, passion, and joy.

Neuroscience of this century is helping us understand why for many of us going to talk therapy and drudging up misery in order to feel better simply hasn't worked. While it has certainly been beneficial for some, for others, like me, it hasn't helped us feel better in the long run. In fact, as happened with Luke, going to talk therapy sometimes makes things worse. Remembering and talking about painful experiences can stress out the brain-body, thereby further degenerating the neurons in the hippocampus that are specific to self-regulation. That's obviously not what we want! Whether we're talking about the problem in therapy or venting to a friend, focusing our attention on the problem can make it feel bigger. That's just how the brain works. We need to spend less time talking (especially about our worries) and more time in the *experience* of relief, balance, and peace. That way, the brain-body learns how to "do" relief, balance, and peace. It's that simple. Our brain-body learns from having the experience, not from talking about wanting to have the experience, or being sick of not having the experience, or making a plan for some future date when the experience will finally happen.

We need to stop talking and simply have the experience. Go on. Give it to yourself right now. You only need 60 Seconds. ☺

Thanks to the neuroscience, we are realizing that although talk therapy can be helpful for some, many of us get better more quickly without it. The same goes for medication. While it can be helpful, and may even be necessary for some people, others of us experience terrible side effects that leave us feeling hopeless. When we don't feel great taking medication, but we've been convinced that we won't get better without medication, life can get pretty grim. Enter the good news again: there's another way! 60 Seconds can quickly bring the brain-body to its antidotal, more natural state of well-being, in a shorter span of time than it takes to find our pill bottle, pour a glass of water, and take the pill! When we sit, stand, or lie in the physiological state that 60 Seconds creates, we are in the more grounded, peaceful place that releases the same neurochemistry in the brain that is in the pill, whatever the pill is. I'm telling you! Do I need to insert a cartwheel here?!

Our brain-body naturally produces the neurotransmitters that are synthetically manufactured and put into anti-depressants, such as dopamine and serotonin. With the help of 60 Seconds, even when our brain-body is out of practice and not producing these neurotransmitters in a high enough concentration for a pleasure response, we can trigger their production to once again stir up all their soothing effects. And, you don't have to find time to do so! Use whichever of the tools you can while driving, sitting at the auto club or hair salon, taking a shower, or sitting at your desk drafting a memo. Soon enough (after 21-28 times), the brain-body remembers how to produce these physiological changes automatically with little to no help at all. That's what it means to rewire the brain, and that's what it means to be free. Everything you need is *in* you, and with you all the time, wherever you are.

This does not mean we promptly go off our medications and do 60 Seconds instead. I am now inserting the necessary disclaimer. Here it is:

Please don't take yourself off the medications that are keeping you alive! NOT my message! Aside from potentially hurting you, that could get me in a whole lot of trouble. What to do, rather, as I did for myself and have done for numerous clients and students, is build the neural pathways for greater self-regulation by doing 60 Seconds over and over again WHILE remaining, for now, on the medication(s). Once those neural pathways are strong, from at least 21-28 experiences with 60 Seconds, then we may be able to slowly wean off the medication(s). The important ingredient here is observation. We must notice each day how we are feeling, and respond accordingly. This is essential throughout the process. (Let your physicians know what you're up to, please!)

For myself, and many of my clients and students, it has been important to add regular exercise and healthy eating or natural supplements that support hormonal and neurochemical balance. There are many varieties on the market today. While many of us can't necessarily get to the gym, we can go skating or for a bike ride with our children. Please do. Our children need the activity and fresh air as much as we do. Anything fun that gets us moving and out in nature produces the physiological responses we need.

Increasing the physical movement of the body has been shown to decrease the over-activity of thought that too often gets centered on what we need to do, what we haven't done, and what we did that wasn't good enough. Moving out of the left brain of thought, into the right brain of movement aids in our capacity to quiet the mind.

Yoga and meditation can quiet the mind, thereby giving us the relief our body craves. Such practices can put us in that same peaceful state needed for neuronal genesis and greater self-regulation. For that reason, I encourage them. However, some yoga and meditation practices can take us out of our body even more, strengthening neural pathways for our disappearing act, as opposed to supporting us to show up in life in a really grounded, present way. That's when I become less encouraging. Please know, however, that if you are able to find the kind of time it takes to meditate or go to a yoga class, and you are feeling yourself becoming more present and grounded as a result, your brain-body loves you for it! If, however, you're like me, and finding that kind of time is difficult, know that 60 Seconds is here for you. Remember, it is a **walking, talking tool** that creates the big changes that come from yoga, mindfulness, and other types of meditation, but in much less time. I often notice my breathing when I am driving my son to school, for example. I notice my feet on the ground when I am talking to audiences. I notice the support of my chair when I am working with clients. We don't need to have all kinds of time, that ever-elusive "alone time," or the perfect place to sit and be quiet, in order to give our brain-body what it needs right now to heal itself. 60 Seconds resets the brain-body to feel relief, come into greater balance, and grow in its capacity to self-regulate big emotions *any* old time!

Utilizing as many healthy tools as often as possible will increase the likelihood of quicker and greater results. That's why 60 Seconds is comprised of *five* tools. Everything works together. If one tool doesn't kick in at first, the others are there to help. If we struggle with feeling our feet on the ground in one particular moment of trying, we can simply move our focus to breathing in through our nose and not worry about our feet for that moment. Eventually, from repeated attempts that focus only on the tools that come into our awareness quickly and with ease, all the tools begin to work. The point is that 60 Seconds is its own little toolkit. It's right there inside of us, and it comes at no cost. These two facts alone mean that once we've got 60 Seconds working for us, we can be free from the worry over whether or not our usual ways of soothing with external resources are available to us or not. Let me give you an example:

When I asked a client of mine what she uses to feel

better when she needs to, she said, "Sleep."

"Good, " I said. "I love my sleep. It's so important and good for resetting the balance of our nervous system. What else?"

"The shower," she said.

"Yum. Yeah," I said (and yes, this is how I talk). "What else?"

"The computer," she said. "Or television."

"That probably helps you escape and forget momentarily about the stress and pressure of it all, huh?"

"Yes," she agreed.

"Okay. I love that you have these things to help you, and I love that right now they're working for you. What do you do when you are stuck somewhere and you can't get to any of these things?"

PANIC! (See her eyes popping out of her head. That's what it looked like.)

Did I really induce a state of panic in my client? That doesn't sound very therapeutic, does it? Bad doctor! I promise, I kept true to my word: my office *is* the place to come to in order to feel good now. Long before I asked these questions, I had prompted my client at the beginning of the session to "marinate" in the soothing physiological effects of 60 Seconds. Her internal resources (the tools of 60 Seconds) were at her disposal, so she remained regulated in spite of feeling triggered briefly by my suggestion. That's what we want: the calming effects of our tools to kick in automatically from inside of us. We don't want to set up a pattern of coping that isn't there for us when we need it the most. What would be the point of that? I explained to my client, as I am to you, I want us to have everything we need *inside of us* so that no matter where we are or how stuck we feel, we have what it takes at our disposal to regulate back to the good feeling place with ease. *That* is freedom, and that level of freedom is *power*.

Without knowing this effective set of tools, most of us have set up a pattern of coping that involves escape or a pattern of plowing through days and weeks and then scheduling a vacation from real life to get temporary relief. We don't need to anymore. We don't even need to go to the spa for hours at a time or take any other form of "mini-vacation" from our lives (although these are fun things to do out of wanting, not needing). The point is that escaping from our real life doesn't help us learn ways to be *in* our lives feeling good. It's a pattern that doesn't help our children either.

What are we teaching our children as they watch and experience with us these all-or-nothing patterns? We teach them "zero-ten-ing"—that all too familiar rollercoaster ride we can't seem to get off. The "ten" is when we plow through life at pretty high voltage, checking off our to-do lists while our head rolls on the floor. The "zero" is when we crash, sometimes checking out with some form of self-medication. Notice the difference in the diagram below between The Zone, which is our 4-7 range when we are self-regulated and fabulous, and the more extreme ranges of response when we are out of The Zone and not so fabulous.

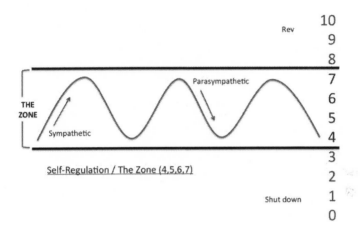

Self-Regulation / The Zone (4,5,6,7)

Part of why we continue to do things the old way, more extremely, in a way that doesn't feel great, at least not in the long run, is because we're not sure old dogs learn new tricks. We may believe that it's too late to be any different. Remember those "critical periods" in development we've been told about? Something needs to happen in just the right way at just the right time by just the right person; if not, it is too late to do anything about it. Our repetitive patterns of behavior over time are what we have used as evidence that this must be true. We can't really change what we do. We've tried. We wanted to stop smoking; we wanted to stop drinking; we wanted to stop shopping when we can't afford to, and yet we keep doing it. Surely, this is proof that we can't undo the way our brains were wired a long time ago.

Not so, says recent neuroscience. We now know more definitively that the brain possesses a most exciting quality called neuroplasticity. This means that experience builds new neural pathways *throughout the lifespan*, no matter how "old" we are or how long we've been doing it another way. We don't need to have had love and affection from our parents to know love and affection in our lives now. We can begin to focus on the love and affection that is available to us in this moment with the person in front of us in this moment. When we notice and focus on that, neurons fire to create neural pathways that support more of that experience. It becomes something we notice more, focus on more, become more comfortable with, and allow in our lives in a bigger way.

The neuroscientist Richard Davidson has stated that he focuses NOT on fixing what we think is wrong or lacking, no matter what the condition, be it ADHD or anything else.[5] Rather, he focuses on "revising our mind with life-enriching experiences." Don't focus on NOT smoking, for example. Simply do 60 Seconds as often as you can to rewire your brain-body for greater self-regulation so that smoking naturally, and on its own, becomes less and less necessary. Right now, we self-medicate to self-regulate; soon enough, with 60 Seconds, we won't need our drug of choice to self-medicate *or self-regulate.* We'll be more physiologically, naturally able to enjoy a glass of wine, a videogame, a television show, or anything else with moderation and peace. Self-regulation for moderation is what frees us at last.

The more often we experience the good feelings we get from these tools, the more neural pathways we have for those good feelings to start taking over. We begin to gravitate towards more of what brings about those good feelings in a healthy way, and we gravitate less towards the temporary fix.

This new path of painless, convenient intervention lowers blood pressure, heart rate, and cortisol levels.[6] It changes lives—completely. Instead of needing to escape from our real, day-to-day life, we now get to be *in* it having a different, healthier experience *of* it—one that is more grounded and balanced, less stressful and overwhelming.

Playtime

The next chapter will teach more about the first tool of 60 Seconds. Here, I simply want to introduce the first tool in an experiential way. Let's begin by noticing the effects on our brain-body of feeling solid ground. That way we will begin to *experience* a physiological change rather than read about how nice it would be to have one someday.

Right now, if your legs are crossed, uncross them and place your feet flat on the ground. If you're in bed, bend your knees up and put your feet flat on the bed. Notice this: your feet are flat on the surface beneath them. If you are having a hard time feeling them connected or grounded, simply wiggle your toes and/or press your heels into the surface below. Go back and forth, pushing in one foot and then the other, wiggling your toes, noticing what the surface feels like beneath your feet. We are simply igniting the firing of neurons that will grow in strength the more we have the experience. Don't worry if the physical sensation of solid ground under your feet isn't coming to you quickly. Soon enough, it will. We are just beginning.

This week, all I would like you to do, and this is really important, is to begin to notice the times, however brief, when you are *in* The Zone, NOT "zero-ten-ing" but feeling less racy and more calm, less anxious and more content. You may notice moments when you are communicating well at work, getting along with a co-worker, laughing with your child or partner, feeling the sun on your face, or how good it feels to sit. Simply take note of these moments, paying attention to what the physical sensations are inside your body when you are more regulated in this way. Perhaps your jaw isn't as clenched, your shoulders are more relaxed, or your belly feels more open. See if in these moments you can notice your feet on the ground. Read on for the science behind the importance of noticing your feet on the ground. This underused and invaluable first tool of 60 Seconds moves us toward ridding ourselves of unwanted habits and building neural pathways for more long-term and healthy fun!

2
Tool One:
Solid Ground

Okay, we now know that re-wiring the brain begins by having an experience. Let's move from knowing or "getting it" on a cognitive level to knowing and "getting it" inside our brain-body. We will begin in this moment by asking ourselves the simple question, "Are my feet flat on the ground?" When we ask ourselves this, we look for the answer. We give our attention to our feet to see if in fact they are on the ground; and if they are, we notice this, and when we notice this, a little message goes off in our brain that instantaneously lowers our blood pressure.[7] It's as if our brain says, "Awww...yes...my feet are planted on solid ground." When our feet are flat, and our blood pressure goes down, our brain and body get to have a break from working so hard.

High blood pressure is a sign that our body is working overtime to pump blood in and out of our heart and throughout the whole of us. This is taxing on all the parts of our integrated brain-body. When nurses check our blood pressure, they will tell us to uncross our legs and put our feet flat on the floor in order to get a better blood pressure reading (or at least they're supposed to). Right now, please wiggle your toes and simply notice that your feet are planted on the ground.

When armed service men and women begin their basic training, they are taught to wiggle their toes in order to more readily feel their feet on the ground. A teacher at one of my educational seminars taught me this. He had just returned to the classroom after serving in the war in Afghanistan and was excited to learn the neuroscientific reason his training officers had focused on this so persistently. Wiggling our toes brings our attention to our feet, which helps increase our awareness that they are more securely connected to whatever surface we're on. This "grounds the live wire" of our energy, in electrical terms. The "live wire" is the arousal or anxiety provoked by stressful situations. Putting our feet flat on the ground calms the electrical current of that live wire and shifts it back into balance so stress is tolerable rather than overwhelming. Have you ever seen an actual live wire? It's wild and out of control. You haven't ever fit this description have you? (Me neither.) Your child maybe? (No. Mine's an angel too.)

I know many of us don't believe that living our daily lives is akin to combat, but more and more, our brain-body processes the rapid overstimulation with which we are bombarded as though we are fighting for our lives. The part of the brain that responds to stress the quickest is primitive. It isn't sophisticated enough to slow down and analyze what kind of stress it is under in order to appropriate a response. It just goes into a survival type of response automatically. It errs on the side of caution, as it is hard-wired from birth to do. Survival is the primary purpose of the brain, to be ensured at all costs.

Running on survival energy can, over time, make us crazy or sick unless we know what to do about it. Electricians know the only thing we can do with a live wire to calm it and make it useful again is to ground it. As simple as it sounds, noticing our feet on the ground does exactly that. Our jitters, anxiety, restlessness, fear, and racy nerves begin to calm. Professional athletes are trained to do this in order to perform at their very best. When basketball players are at the free throw line, they need to settle their nerves in order to make the shot. Take a look next time at what they do in order to improve their performance. They take about 60 seconds (or less) to perform a little ritual, don't they? They shift their weight from one foot to the other because that way they can feel the weight of their feet on the ground underneath them, supporting their body to be more stable and balanced on the flat floor below. They move from side to side, noticing their feet on the court, breathing in through their nose, visualizing the success of their shot, and then they take it—with far more success and with far greater ease when using their tools than when not using them. It's a lot like that in life.

We all need to know how to keep cool under pressure, how to have our "right mind about us" in order to execute our finest performance, and to make the best decisions possible, no matter how much stress we are under. The work I do with parents and teachers illustrates this. What job is more stressful than taking care of kids?! As much as I love children, my own included, I can relate to my teacher clients when they say they want to stick their students "in a washing machine that has a spin cycle from here to hell." (That's a mild one.)

We naturally find ourselves fantasizing about payback, don't we? That's what happens when we aren't using our tools. When we are grounded, consciously aware that our feet are solidly planted, we instantaneously begin to feel all the benefits of lower blood pressure, and that often means no one ends up dead. That's a good thing. With lowered blood pressure, our heart rate lowers, and this deepens our breathing. In turn, our muscles relax and together, all of this moves us into what some neuroscientists aptly call the "yes brain," a more fluid, expanded neural state that promotes focus and supports the fullness of life. In this state, we surprisingly become aware of more choices. Our thinking becomes more agile and creative. When we are in this good-feeling state, the *parasympathetic* branch of the autonomic nervous system—the part that soothes and calms—is active and dominant. This branch is essential for self-regulation.

Unlike the "yes brain," the "no brain" is the result of an active and dominant *sympathetic* branch of the autonomic nervous system. Just think of this branch as the one that revs us up. It leaves us feeling like we're floating, disconnected from solid ground, filled with anxiety, high blood pressure, tension, and so on. This is a tighter, less flexible state that largely focuses on survival. Not very sympathetic, is it?

If we were stressed all the time without the parasympathetic balancing out our experience, our more primitive, sensory, nonverbal brain, the brain stem, would rule. And when it does, it chooses either a fight, flight, or freeze response. Much of what we are recognizing as problematic in our culture today, whether at home with out of control partners or children, or in schools with out of control teachers or students, is that most of us at one time or another, with the slightest provocation, will go into one of these three responses: fight, flight, or freeze. This is how we have learned to "cope" – to survive – but it is not how we thrive and live a most joyful, healthy life. We need to get grounded for that possibility. A grounded nervous system is one that can experience stress in a tempered way—the balance between the sympathetic and parasympathetic—so that huge "ten" responses like the "live wire," as well as "zero" responses like "shut down," are less likely.

Numerous CEOs of Fortune 500 and other high-stakes companies are now required to learn how to meditate or do yoga in order to handle millions, sometimes billions of dollars without making a mistake, just as professional sports teams, like the LA Lakers now make yoga and meditation part of their required training for the year. That's because yoga and meditation quiet the brain-body, as does 60 Seconds – only 60 Seconds takes a lot less time, *and* you can do it standing up. Come on, when's the last time you got to do it *standing up*?! ☺

From astronauts in space to soldiers on the ground, wiggling our toes to become more solidly planted helps us take back the part of our brain that gets hijacked by stress—the part of the brain that is more rational, reasonable, logical, linear, analytical, and capable of making excellent decisions. Better yet, the balance in the brain and nervous system that is restored by becoming more consciously grounded is what integrates the whole brain, left and right, the more analytical with the more creative, so we can problem-solve more flexibly, think outside the box more creatively, reason more critically, and come up with the kinds of new ideas that are going to keep us moving forward on this planet in an innovative, empathic, humanistic, and more socially responsible way. Phew! That was an exciting mouthful.

Recess

Right now, in order to take a break from the words and practice getting grounded, let's use a visual aid: imagine that you are standing at the beach, down at the tide, where the sand is a little wet from waves ebbing and flowing. As you stand in wet sand, notice how you sink down an inch or two with the sand enveloping your feet, giving you the sensation of being a little "sunk in." If that doesn't work for you, you can imagine that growing out from the bottom of your feet are roots, like the roots of a tree, spreading out in every direction and as deep down into the earth's core as you would like to imagine. See the earth's color and texture, like rich chocolate, cool, moist and full of nutrients, vitamins, and oxygen. Imagine all that good stuff coming up and into you through your feet, nourishing your body and brain with all that you need for health and well-being. As you imagine one or the other visual, focus on becoming more securely planted to Mother Earth. Her resources are here for us to feel more supported as we journey this physical plane.

When I first begin grounding others—clients, students, parents, and educators—I find that, for many, the relief is immediate. For others of us, it takes a little longer for the neural pathways to develop as noticeably. We may be able to focus on our feet or the visual for only a few seconds at a time at first, but each time we do, neurons fire, neural pathways are formed, and soon enough we find we can focus for 30 seconds at a time, then 60 seconds. Everyone gets "there"—to that place of noticing greater relief and ease and, if not immediately, before you know it, smiles happen, faces soften, shoulders drop, and one of the most important resources in life is restored: hope.

The best teacher I know, Ms. Susan, always tells her students, "If you're not getting it, you will." Isn't that the most loving thing to say? And when they do "get it," it dawns on them sometimes for the first time, when they begin to feel safe in their own body, that maybe they'll be okay. Maybe they are okay, at least in this moment, and if they can be okay in this moment, then maybe it's possible to have more moments like this one. Many I have worked with over the years soon began to feel okay again without their drug of choice. We are all skeptical at first, of course. This is too simple, and too good to be true. We say: *How is it that no one has ever shown me something so simple before? This has to be a fluke or short-term or impossible to do on my own. What's the catch to this? I sit here for 60 seconds and notice a few things happening, and I feel as good as I do when I smoke a joint? But wait a minute, it's even better because I'm actually present. I'm here un-buzzed, un-checked-out – checked in and feeling good?*

The first time I did 60 Seconds with one of the gang members I worked with at Reid High School, an alternative high school in Long Beach, CA, the student looked his body up and down in disbelief after I asked him what he was noticing inside. He replied with apparent astonishment, "I haven't even smoked one yet." *How can I be feeling so chill so quickly without my marijuana?* The same kind of response came from the father of one of the teenagers I worked with in private practice. I require parents to experience the tools I teach their children so they can understand how and why they are so effective. I require parents to start using the tools themselves to better assist their child in making the improvements everyone wants to see. We can't expect our children to get better if we are still walking around the house with stress oozing out of our pores. As is true with all my child and adolescent clients, in this particular case, I knew the gains I was having with this teenage boy would be vulnerable if the parents did not take good care of themselves. After all, we are inextricably linked, every one of us, especially when we live in close quarters. We affect each other in healthy or unhealthy ways depending upon how well regulated our own nervous system is. We soak up each other's energy in very palpable ways. When I asked the father what he noticed happening inside his body after doing 60 Seconds he said, dreamily, "I feel like I just had four cocktails." I said, "Exactly. Except you can actually leave here anytime you want and drive home. How great is that?"

We are all using something to help us cope with the ever-increasing demands of our life, whether it's marijuana, alcohol, food, or something else. Some people gamble; others shop; some hoard; others use television, videogames, pornography, orgasms, exercise, cutting, binge eating, smoking, starving, or raging with anger. Whatever it is, and depending upon what it is, it may be completely fine in moderation. Such approaches stop working, however, when they begin to take up our time, money, energy, and mind space, *and* when they begin to agitate us. Ironically, our pacifier stops being a source of genuine soothing in various scenarios: if it's out of reach somehow and we can't get to it; when we've done too much; or, when we feel the shame of realizing that we aren't controlling it anymore, it's controlling us.

What's beautiful about 60 Seconds is we needn't declare ourselves an addict or powerless over an "addiction" in order to begin getting the help we need. In fact, the neuroscience is helping us get clearer about how labeling, like calling someone an "addict," can have undesirable effects. Identifying and focusing on "problems" to be fixed puts our focus in the wrong place. "What we focus on expands" used to be considered a bit of a woo-woo metaphysical truth. We now know, however, that it is also a neuroscientific fact. What we focus on causes corresponding neurons in the brain to fire. When we continue to focus on whatever we are focusing on, corresponding neurons fire more intensely, thereby finding one another to form strong neural connections that become deeply embedded in our brain structure. These deeply imbedded neural connections lead to corresponding behaviors that become automatic.

So, when we focus on having healthy experiences and we begin to fill up more and more of our day with those healthier thoughts, behaviors, and rituals—like 60 Seconds—our healthier neural connections get stronger. Neural pathways for the problem that we have had neither the time nor inclination to focus on anymore become weaker. Eventually, "ignored" or "avoided" problems, ideas, thoughts and their corresponding neural pathways die off, a process called "neural pruning."

When people try to make us feel as though ignoring or avoiding a problem is a bad thing, please give them an education in neuroscience. Sometimes, it's the best thing we can do. Enough with the negative connotations to these words! There are times when there is nothing wrong with ignoring or avoiding a problem, especially when what we're actually doing is refocusing. What *is* "wrong"—or at least a drag—is not making the choice to-rewire the brain by doing more healthy things that feel good, especially when they take only seconds to do. I completely relate to not wanting to "*work*" at "fixing a problem" or having to reduce the use of something that brings us greater calm. That sounds painful and hard. I want to be done with self-improvement that's painful and hard. Good thing it no longer has to be! We only do well when we feel *good*, and we just don't feel good when we dwell on a problem.

Consider this: We may not need to concern ourselves with reducing our self-medication of choice; we may be better off instead by doing 60 Seconds everyday. The more we do it, the easier it becomes, and the easier it becomes, the more we do it. The more we do it, the better we feel, and the better we feel, the better we do. It's that simple! (Insert fireworks. That's actually IT in a nutshell folks, but please keep reading anyway. ☺) 60 Seconds leads to more of the good feelings that reduce our need for self-medication as much or as often. Why worry about perfect abstinence when we can, *with ease*, regulate our body back into greater balance for moderation?

I can hear the 12-Steppers up in arms right now! Please, hear me when I say if you have found an approach to your life that works, keep doing it. I respect each individual person's choice for how to live his or her life when it isn't hurting anyone. Having said that, if a 12-step program has not worked for you because abstinence is not something you could possibly imagine (or for any other reason), I am here to tell you I understand (quite personally!) and so does the neuroscience. We can't take away a coping mechanism without replacing it with something else that works just as easily and quickly, that feels just as good. (And I don't think cigarettes are what we really want replacing alcohol, for example. We want to be healthy!) Many of us have noticed that we can't replace our drug of choice and the quick, albeit temporary relief it brings with something that takes longer to do, or something that brings relief *eventually*...We need to feel good now! And I'm not sure dogma is doin' it for us. If it is, fabulous, but if you need a little tool to go along with your dogma, I'm your gal.

Some people can white-knuckle it at first. They can abstain from the behavior and thereby prune those neural pathways for self-medication. I applaud those who are living a healthy life having done it that way, with or without a 12-step program. What I am offering with **60 Seconds is an alternative to the abstinence model. It gradually replaces self-medication with the most** invaluable INTERNAL resource of all—self-regulation.

When the use of our "drug" of choice does not interfere with our relationships, our work, or any other facet of our life, such as self-development, then it's simply an enjoyment of one of the pleasures of life. When we use in excess as a way to medicate feelings that are difficult, as a way to disconnect from someone or something that's hard or painful, or as a way to stay in an unhealthy relationship or job, using falls into the category of self-medication. This is the kind of use that stunts our self-development and hurts our children. Overuse is what cuts us off from all we are meant to be, and all we can be for our children and the people we love.

What we forget over time as we use our distraction of choice to quiet or numb the uncomfortable, whether we experience the uncomfortable as boredom, self-loathing, loneliness, mania, hyperactivity, or fear, is that we have the power to do it another way. While 12-step programs may work for many, for others of us, the first step of declaring ourselves powerless doesn't help, and it's not supported by the neuroscience. We may have forgotten how powerful we really are; we may need to be reminded through healthy experiences of our power, but we're certainly not powerless. It even says so in the Bible, in the book of Corinthians: change doesn't come from words; it comes from power.[8] We need to claim and feel our power in order to make healthy, life-long changes. We do this by focusing on the good choices we've made before, the power we had to make those better choices, and the pleasant feelings we experienced as a result.

I offer an important study to make my point. I believe it is one of the most important studies of our time, and that it will become one of the most influential, certainly in mental health, and hopefully in education and parenting if I have anything to do with it. According to a *Los Angeles Times* article,[9] the University of Southern California (USC) conducted a study involving three groups. All the participants were told that each person in each group would have his or her turn to go into a room with a piece of chocolate cake. The control group was given no further instructions or information. They were simply put in the room, one by one, with the piece of chocolate cake. In the second group, everyone was told to go into the room, one at a time, each for his or her own turn to focus on the last time he or she ate too much chocolate cake. They were directed to concentrate on how they felt, how much they regretted it and how their doctor had cautioned them not to eat so many sweets because of health-related issues. (I'm paraphrasing to give the general flavor of what they were told to focus on.) The third group was told to go into the room with the piece of chocolate cake and focus on the last time they chose *not* to eat so much cake. They were instructed to remember when they chose to savor a few bites then let the rest go so they could get into their jeans and feel good about their choice.

At the end of the experiment, which group do we think ate the most chocolate cake? Do we need to think about it or do we know immediately, from a gut feeling perhaps, or what makes the most sense? In this experiment, the group that ate the most cake was the group that focused on the bad feelings they experienced from remembering a time they made a bad choice, from remembering a loss of power and self-control. The group that ate the least chocolate cake was the group that focused *not* on bad feelings from mistakes made, but on the good feelings that came from remembering their own power.

Good feelings release the perfect biochemical "soup" in the brain-body to give it the juice it needs to do the healthier thing. When our brain and nervous system are depleted of "happy chemicals," when we experience a surge of "unhappy biochemistry" from remembering powerlessness and shame, we have less of what we need in the brain-body to make the more desirable choice. Remember, what we focus on expands.

Focus on bad feelings and you get more bad feelings. Who can stand feeling bad? Soon enough, we're eating chocolate cake so we can't feel that we're feeling bad! We behave in a way that will give us, albeit temporarily, relief from the bad feelings. Focus on the good feelings that come from remembering healthier choices, and we create inside of us the physiological power necessary for making a better choice in the future. Even if we've never made a healthy choice before, we can imagine what it would look and feel like to do so, and when we do, neurons fire in our brain as though we are actually having the experience. This causes a surge of "happy chemicals" that help us do well. Now, that's mind power!

The Chocolate Cake Study has far reaching consequences for our educational and parenting practices. Right now, we are convinced that if we make someone feel badly enough about what they've done, surely they will never do it again. Right? The logical, linear left brain says, "Right! Once we make this person feel deaf, dumb, and blind, they'll feel *determined* to pick themselves up and succeed." The more primitive, animal brain that needs us to thrive says, "Hell to the no!" It doesn't work that way for any of us. Have you noticed? Beating ourselves up does the opposite of what we want it to do. It doesn't help us to stop behaving in the ways that later bring us shame. Feeding powerlessness and shame feeds the proverbial beast that lives in each one of us—the physiological state of discomfort that causes us to behave in ways we later regret.

The Chocolate Cake Study has two important messages: 1) Stop shaming, punishing, criticizing, and focusing on the problem – and I mean this for all of us. It doesn't work. It does the opposite of what we want it to do. 2) Focus instead, every chance we get, on the times when the problem *doesn't* exist or *didn't* exist, when things *feel* right, better, and healthier or *felt* right, better, and healthier. Focus instead on what we are doing when things are going well, or on what we were doing when things were going better. Concentrate on the healthier choices we are making presently or on the healthier choices we've made in the past, as well as the good feelings that those choices create. We all need to do this for ourselves first, then for our partner, our children, our employees, our colleagues. Then, just like magic, the pixie dust will have been sprinkled in just the right way and poof! When we ground ourselves, not in our bad feelings but in the ones that make us happy to be alive, we begin to get more of what we *really* want.

Playtime

Right now focus on feeling your two feet flat on the floor, the ground, the bed, or the earth. Use the visual suggested during Recess, earlier in the chapter, of standing on the wet sand or having roots growing out from the bottom of your feet. If you can't easily feel them on the surface below, that's okay, simply wiggle your toes or push in your heels, using the visual at the same time. Begin to notice how you feel inside. You may feel things slowly calming down, dropping, settling, sinking, or getting heavier. You may begin to feel more secure, more connected, or more supported by solid ground. When you do, you will have the beginning of what we all need in order to live free of everything external to us. You will be liberated to experience the power that is alive and well *within* you, even if it is muted at the moment.

This week, anytime you are standing in line, at the DMV perhaps, grocery store, or bank, be conscious about feeling gravity at work. Feel all of your weight on your feet on the ground beneath you. Move your weight from one foot to the other to notice how balanced and stable you are with two strong feet and legs supporting you. That's all. Every chance you get this week, in situations where you find yourself waiting in a line, use that time to bring your awareness to your feet planted on the ground.

3

Tool Two:
Support Right Here, Right Now

Support is something we expect to come from people. Not just any people. From the people we love, and the people who love us. That's just logical and linear. It makes sense. So how's it working? Are we feeling supported? Not so much...?

I know. The problem is, the people we want and expect support from, are living in the same Nutsville we are. If they're not, they're surrounded by people who *are*! No one is stress-free. In fact, we are more stressed in Western culture than we have ever been. We are working harder, longer hours, commuting farther, juggling careers and family life, achieving financially, losing financially, all while texting and Tweeting, often at the same time. Combine all of this, and we are swirling up and out like the wild nature of the live wire. We try to ground our frenetic tailspin by connecting with others, but it's like the Tasmanian Devil meeting the Roadrunner. This is not good for the planet. It's not grounding to get together on a sinking ship, even if you believe misery loves company. No, thank you. If my choices are to die miserably with other people, or die peacefully alone, I'll take the latter, thank you.

Having said that, needing to feel supported is part of the human experience. We are social beings who, by nature, are interdependent for the purposes of survival. When we are supported, we feel good, and when we feel good, we do well. When we do well we thrive, and when we thrive, we survive. This is basic biology. Support, however, does not have to come from people in order for it to be considered "support," or for it to have its beneficial effects. This realization, for me, was a Hallelujah moment.

I remember an analogy that came from none other than Dr. Phil, and it helped me understand why I didn't love spending time with my sister, even though I wanted to be able to have a relationship with her. I came to recognize that depending upon my sister for "support" was easy enough. She liked inviting me, hosting me, feeding me, and showing me what was going on in her life. She had a beautiful home and good food and nice things. All I had to do in return for her generous hospitality was stick my hand in a blender.

This is an analogy, remember. ☺

So I would. Though we didn't like each other much and rarely felt good in each other's company, I could hear my brain checking off from the to-do list of right and appropriate things to do: "Have a relationship with my sister. Check." And all I had to do was stick my hand in her blender. No problem.

Wrong.

Problem.

I'm grateful for 60 Seconds in a way that I don't think I'll ever be able to explain. I discovered, through the use of these tools, that I don't need my sister's "support," and I certainly don't need her blender. All I need is my own self-regulation. Check.

If you've had enough of being disappointed by the behavior of people who are as overscheduled, overwhelmed, and stressed as you are, remember, there is another way. Counting on other people, or anything else external to us, can bring about too much disappointment too often. Mount enough of these frustrating experiences, combined with the expectation that people *should* be supporting us, and we begin to feel more and more alone. We may even find ourselves wanting to give up. Feeling alone and unsupported, especially when we focus on these emotions, feeds the bad feelings I was talking about in Chapters One and Two. As we now know, if we didn't know already, bad feelings lead us to behave in ways we aren't proud of because when we do, we at least achieve momentary relief from the feelings.

When we do 60 Seconds, however, and we begin to notice the support of what we are sitting, lying, or standing in (and I do mean "in"), we prime the brain to notice more of the support that is around us everywhere, anywhere, in *any* given moment. We may never have experienced it that way before. Instead, we may have a story in our head that goes something like, "Support needs to come from people and if it isn't coming from people, then we don't have support." Not so. Call a spade a spade. Support simply *is* support – whether it's from Mother Nature or from sitting on the toilet bowl. Notice now that while you are sitting in whatever you're in, it is holding you up, doing the work, preventing you from falling to the ground, offering your back support at times, and anchoring your bottom. (Let's be off the toilet bowl visual for that one.)

Now notice your bottom as an anchor. Gravity causes all your weight to be absorbed by your bottom, giving it a really solidly planted, weighted sensation. When you allow yourself to bring that solid feeling into your awareness, as well as the support of what you're sitting in, you realize that you are right now having an experience of support. When we notice that and "take it in," we get relief.

Let's talk about relief, and priming the brain to notice when we are having it. (The toilet bowl image works here again, doesn't it?) The experience of relief, combined with the awareness that we are having it, is the antidote to the effects of stress. It's medicine. Physiologically, relief is our blood pressure lowering, our heart rate decreasing, and our stress hormones, like cortisol, dropping. This is what Xanax and many other drugs, prescribed or illegal, do for us. The tools of 60 Seconds are *natural* drugs. They, too, have a measurable impact on our brain and nervous system. We simply have to notice. *Sensory awareness* or *noticing what is happening inside our body* is the catalyst that creates the magic. Sensory awareness allows the tools to take their effect more quickly and powerfully. Remember, *noticing* the effect of the tools on our body is what causes brain cells or neurons to fire strongly. When they fire strongly, they find each other quickly to form a neural pathway that gets stronger each time the experience occurs.

Noticing support with 60 Seconds is effective because it causes neurons in the brain to fire and form neural pathways or connections for noticing support at other times, no matter where or how we are receiving it. In other words, one experience transfers to another because the brain has been primed. Our brain-body soon begins to notice our grounded feet and our focused breathing (in through the nose, deep into the belly) while we are lying in our bed, walking down the hall, talking to a colleague, or standing in line. Our awareness of support expands to the context we are in. Our definition of support expands to include what is happening in the moment we're in. Soon, we notice the warmth of the sun, the cool comfort of the breeze, the beauty in a work of art, the perfect light coming from our reading lamp. We begin to see and accept all the ways Mother Nature and the rest of our physical environment is offering us support. Experiences in nature, *especially*, just like most experiences with animals, deeply trigger the soothing support of the parasympathetic branch of the nervous system.

Consider the very different way we are working here with 60 Seconds: traditional therapeutic interventions, such as talk therapy, support groups, and 12-step programs are top-down approaches. With top-down approaches, we work with the higher order brain (the neocortex) and the left brain to logically break down what makes sense and what doesn't, so that with our greater insight and understanding we can begin to make better choices. The idea is that if we improve our thoughts, surely our bodies will come along for the ride and make the changes we want. We'll set a goal, identify all the smaller steps that will get us to the goal, and then we'll achieve it. We'll get to the gym, stop smoking, and be kinder in our relationships.

This top-down way of working has for some, unfortunately, produced limited results. We may come to *know* better with this kind of approach, but we often find we still can't *do* better. We've worked with the higher order brain and all of its thoughts, beliefs, and stories in an attempt to make changes there that will fuel what needs to be changed in our physiology. Without altering the more primitive brain, however, to cause a relieving sensory shift in our nervous system, plans don't get executed for long because our body is stuck. It still feels numb, shut down, disconnected, racy, or panicky.

Our ability to execute our plans doesn't come from where we think: the conscious, rational, reasonable brain that analyzes and problem-solves. If it did—as our current mainstream culture would have us believe—then it would be easy to do things differently and get a different result. The reason we often repeat the same pattern over and over again is because our behavior is largely driven by our physiology—the physical feelings of our body. These are different from thoughts and emotions. I am not talking about mad, glad, and sad. I am talking about tight, tense, frozen, numb, jumpy, racy, void, hollow, empty, spacey, out-of-body. I am talking about the physiology of our brain-body—how neural pathways have formed because of the experiences we've had.

Our physical sensations are what drive our thoughts, stories, beliefs, judgments, and *choices*. Not the other way around (though thoughts can and do affect physiology). This is the bottom-up perspective. The sensory part of our brain kicks our survival instinct into action more quickly than our cerebral brain has new insights. By the time our higher order brain has figured out we're afraid, we've already run the length of a football field to get away.

Neuroscience has now confirmed what William James taught as far back as 1890! Our physical sensations and their corresponding impulses come first.[10] The more primitive brain stem lights up *first*, providing sensory information to the higher order brain, which leads the neocortex to form a judgment about the physical sensations. I shiver, therefore I must be cold. I run, therefore I must be afraid. During a panic attack, the physical sensations of a tight chest, difficulty breathing, or racing heart lead the neocortex to make a judgment in response to those physical sensations. Our neocortex might say, *Oh my god! I can't breathe; I'm going to die!* And that's what causes the panic.

Clients who experience panic attacks are helped by 60 Seconds because it soothes the part of the brain that causes scary physical sensations—the amygdala. Though we may notice a tight chest, difficulty breathing, or racing heart, we can also notice our feet on the ground and the support of the couch. These sensory tools provide balance to the physical event, allowing a new experience of it. When we are helped to focus on feeling grounded and supported, the less comfortable physical sensations begin to dissipate, and we notice that they can feel more manageable, less overwhelming, and temporary.

If we want quicker results in life, we need to work with the quicker part of our brain that more automatically decides what kind of choice we're going to make based upon sensations, not feelings or thoughts. We need an approach that soothes, repairs, heals, and releases the physical experiences that keep us stuck—the tight, tense, frozen, numb, jumpy, racy, void, hollow, empty, spacey, out-of-body feelings that drive us, at all costs sometimes, to get relief from it all.

60 Seconds is a bottom-up approach that restores the body's natural balance of ebb and flow. When this natural fluidity, flexibility, and agility is restored back to the nervous system, watch how easily new choices for a different way of being become executed. We have to soothe the body's physiology *first* so that new ways of thinking, telling

a story, believing, and behaving become the natural extension of our state of ease. Taking in the support that is present in any given moment is one valuable way to bring about this greater state of ease in the body, which then enables us to more easily and naturally make a different choice.

Curtis

When Curtis, a young adult and student, came into my office the first time, he let me know that he had gotten all he was going to get out of his educational experience, and that among the other problems that come from wanting to drop out of school, he was "an insomniac." (Most clients come in citing one label or another – what I call "the box.") For years, it had taken him long, torturous hours to fall asleep, and if he woke up in the night, he would struggle to fall back asleep. His lack of sleep was interfering with the quality of his life in general, and his relationships more specifically. He once had a therapist, a well-intentioned man that Curtis liked. They met regularly, and talked about what Curtis could do differently to get a different result—standard therapy that, in the end, brought about no lasting change to the quality of Curtis' life.

I wasted no time talking at length with Curtis about anything. I knew that talking would not change his nervous system, a nervous system that was clearly revved in front of me as we spoke. Both his legs bounced incessantly. I led Curtis through the tools of 60 Seconds, beginning with grounding and taking in the support of the couch, visualizing roots growing out from the bottom of his feet into the earth, inviting him to imagine being securely connected to Her bigness and solidity. This was followed by breath in through the nose. When I asked Curtis what he noticed inside, he reported that in parts of his body he was getting calmer, and in other parts he felt "a jitteriness" that he felt "all the time." I asked Curtis to observe the jitteriness—where it was in his body—and to notice where in his body it was not. I invited him to focus there—on the parts of his body that were feeling calmer so he could describe in greater detail what he was noticing about the calm. Was it a solid, smooth, fluid, warm, or loose feeling? I asked him to be an "observer" of his physical sensations, to see what might happen next.

"When you simply observe your more pleasant sensations with curiosity, what do you become aware of?" I asked. After just a moment of attention, he noticed that the physical sensations he focused on expanded to other parts of his body. I made him aware that he was having a palpable experience of the metaphysical truth, "What we focus on expands." I explained how this is also a neuroscientific fact.

On that first meeting, Curtis and I spent approximately 30 to 40 minutes experiencing the tools of 60 Seconds. I did a little talking about the neuroscience behind the tools, but mostly, we sat together, quietly using our tools. I guided him, with very few words, to help him stay focused on his sensory experience of being grounded, anchored, and supported. He reported feeling more and more calm as we continued, and wondered if he would fall asleep. Because of the "zero-ten-ing" that gets hardwired into the brain, we get used to either being completely revved or passed out. As his rev lessened, he assumed he would pass out, and go from one extreme to the other as he usually did. He did not. He experienced himself as more fully relaxed than he could remember while being in a waking state (what I call, "the new experience").

When Curtis came in the following week, he was amazed and pleased to tell me he had slept all week. He wondered what we had done exactly, and why it was so effective. To help him understand the process, I explained a little more of the neuroscience. It was because he began to notice the support of the couch during our session that he primed his brain to begin to notice the support present in any given moment, such as the bed he lies in while trying to fall asleep. I asked him if he had begun to notice the support of the bed at night, perhaps in a way he had not noticed before. He confirmed this was true. He had started using the tools when he went to bed at night. He described the good feelings that came from his use of them. Those good feelings led him to want to turn his phone and computer off (the new choice) instead of leaving them on at the side of the bed. He had always left them on before, and close to him "in case" anyone tried to reach him in the night. However, Curtis' calmer nervous system from the use of the tools allowed him to make a different choice. His physiological state of relief sent a different message to his brain that said, "What do I need my phone on for?"

This is an example of how working bottom-up as opposed to top-down can be more quickly effective. A top-down behaviorist or cognitive-behaviorist approaching Curtis' insomnia would likely have had him focus on making different choices at night that would theoretically calm his physiological state before sleep, such as turning off his technology an hour or so before getting into bed. This would be one logical, linear choice. Such a suggestion, however, feels threatening to someone like Curtis who escapes from his anxious state with technology. Asking him to give up his way of coping is not relaxing. Curtis was helped by a bottom-up approach. We did not focus on what was wrong with the situation that needed to be changed. Instead, while his technology was left on, Curtis used his tools and they relieved his elevated physiology. Soon he felt enough relief that he didn't need the less healthy way of coping. On his own, he made the different, better choice with ease.

Curtis' commitment to the process grew. We met several more times. At first, he was most comfortable sitting with one leg bent with his foot resting up on the other knee. I didn't concern myself with trying to change that. I simply asked him to feel his one foot planted and to find his anchor, which for him was always the foot that was on the ground. His left foot was the foot on the ground that felt to him the most planted, solid, *and secure* with the weight of his right foot resting on it. As we progressed in our work together, and as I continued to suggest he try having both feet flat on the ground, Curtis began to come in at the beginning of our sessions and automatically sit that way—both feet solidly planted. At the end of our work together, his left foot remained his anchor, but both feet were always flat. Curtis explained that his anchored left foot was the tool that came into his awareness the quickest and the easiest. It was always right there for him, steady and certain. The restless legs that used to shake no longer did. His greater state of calm was obvious to both of us.

Each time Curtis and I met, he came in to report yet another way he was using the tools to achieve a greater quality of life. During one visit, Curtis said he had begun using 60 Seconds in his volleyball games and noticed it improving his performance. Another time, he shared that when he got to class now, one that he couldn't stand being in before, he used his tools for the first two minutes and a new thought came to him - right there in class: "It's only an hour and a half; it can't be that bad." His tolerance had grown. His capacity to make different choices grew out of his greater calm. His new state of ease produced in his mind a new story and belief that the class was only an hour and a half, that it wasn't that bad, and that made it easy for him to engage in different, more acceptable behavior. He no longer bothered the people around him, provoking the teacher into kicking him out. Rather, he was able to sit in his seat and chill. This was a huge shift for Curtis. He was able to get through classes he hadn't been able to stand without *feeling that restlessness in his body, the discomfort, and the anxiety of wanting to get out, or at least act out to distract from sensations that were more challenging. Now his body was less agitated, more calm, and the class more bearable. Nothing about it had changed. What changed was Curtis' nervous system.*

The last time I met with Curtis, he shared that he was openly using his tools while hanging out with his friends in the Jacuzzi. He said his friends thought he was "nuts," but he didn't care. "They're missing out," he said. He radiated from the joy he felt that he was no longer living with constant jitteriness, problems sleeping, and hating being in class. He felt more tolerant of his parents and their differing points of view. He knew they wanted academic results from him within a system he no longer believed in. He knew he couldn't give them what they wanted. But he felt a greater peace with the truth of who he is. He was not going to fit into the picture his parents had painted for him. He was not going to follow in their footsteps of traditional achievement and acquisition. He had long known he was on a different path, and now he had the tools to manage the extreme stress that truth brought. He had what he needed to break free of their dream.

Playtime

Right now, I encourage you to let Curtis' experience lead you to an even greater openness to the tools that have helped him so much. Sit in a chair or on the couch and take in the support it is giving your back and bottom; lean into the back of the chair or couch and rest. Let the chair or couch do the work for you. As you do, see if you can begin to notice a part of you that is sinking in, feeling more weighted or solidly planted than any other part of your body. Your bottom, perhaps, may feel all the weight of the rest of your body upon it and may feel anchored to the seat of the chair or couch as a result. If so, this is what I call your anchor. If not, there may be another part of you, your lower back perhaps, or another part of your back or shoulders leaning into the chair or couch that feels the most planted or anchored. Simply focus on your anchor now, noticing its physical sensations, such as feeling solid or weighted.

As you use this tool of taking in support and finding your anchor, observe yourself with curiosity, noticing your body's inner sensations, to see if your other tool—feeling your feet flat on the ground—becomes more accessible to you. If so, simply focus back and forth on the support of the chair or couch, your anchor weighted, and your feet on the ground. As you do, notice any physical sensations of relief or calm; perhaps a settling, dropping, or sinking sensation; maybe you're getting a little heavier or gradually feeling more securely planted.

If unpleasant sensations are also present, it's okay to notice these. They're just sensations, always temporary if we allow them to be. There is no need to resist them or be afraid of them; simply focus on the parts of you that feel more comfortable, as well as those that feel more securely planted, grounded, and anchored. Sometimes, they are the very same places.

If you are noticing that you are able to do this for just a few seconds and not 60 seconds, that's okay, too. Neural pathways for these tools will grow more quickly than you think; soon the time you are able to focus will increase exponentially.

This week, when you receive a voicemail message, a text, or an email from a colleague, family member, or friend, and it is upsetting to you, please notice that you may be moving out of The Zone of 4-7 and into that less balanced place of "zero-ten-ing." You may notice a tightening in your muscles, a clenching in your jaw, or a constriction in your stomach. These unpleasant physical sensations are speaking to you. They are cuing you to utilize your tools for triggering a more parasympathetic nervous system response. We know how to do that now, though we are still just learning. We do not want to expect these tools to kick in automatically yet, but we do want to begin to consciously make the effort to gradually bring them into our day-to-day experiences.

When you notice the first physical cues of moving out of The Zone in response to an upsetting message from someone, consider bringing your awareness to your feet on the ground, and to any physical support you may have access to in the moment, such as the chair you are sitting in or, if you are outside, the sun on your skin. Thoughts may come into your mind that amp up your system, like stories about the person who has sent the message. Be curious enough to see if you can allow thought, *and yet focus more on sensation*: your feet on the ground and the physical support that is present. Shifting our focus from thought to sensation is tricky at first, but the more we practice, the stronger neural pathways for this new way of being will become.

4

Tool Three:
Like A Good Wine,
We All Need To Breathe

Let's just breathe, shall we? It feels so good! Each time we work with physical sensations that are soothing, we are working in that bottom-up way I mentioned earlier. Once our brain-body is soothed, great stuff can happen, like those changes we've been wanting to make for years! In this chapter, we will learn a very particular way of breathing that is most soothing: in through the nose and deep into the belly. I'll explain why.

Noticing our breath, or any one of the sensory tools of 60 Seconds, helps us to get to the root of it all, what lies beneath our thoughts and feelings—our physiology. We've noticed that we can change our thoughts all we want, recite mantras, state our new intentions for greater peace, but until we soothe the activation of our brain-body from the effects of stress, our words don't create lasting change. It is the stress, pressure, and unresolved trauma of our life that leaves our brain-body in its frenzy. When such experiences are chronic or extreme, they cause over-activation of a part of the brain called the amygdala. When the amygdala becomes triggered by either an accumulation of stress or a significant traumatic event, it buzzes its alarm, releasing hormones and neurotransmitters throughout the brain-body that keep it from feeling good.

Our racing nervous system, driven by the amygdala, overrides our good feelings, causing them to become suppressed or depleted. When we don't feel good, our thoughts become cluttered, urgent, critical, and overwhelming. And yes, these thoughts continue a vicious cycle that keeps the body revved up. (Remember the unsympathetic *sympathetic*?) Does that mean we have to take anti-depressants or anti-anxiety agents to get relief? No. We don't have to use the "medicine" of marijuana either. ☺

Marijuana feels like medicine, doesn't it? For many, it feels like the cure for that ache or pain, that panicky, hyper feeling, or that lack of focus. When stress and/or trauma diminishes the brain-body's natural capacity to soothe itself, all kinds of substances and activities feel like they are "medicine." However, with a little help, the brain-body can produce all that good stuff on its own. Simply, gently, and in an empowering way, we can soothe the amygdala ourselves from the inside. As simple as it sounds, we accomplish this when we consciously breathe in through our nose, deep into the belly. So simple and so beautiful; I want our kids to feel us basking in the joy of it. I want them to see us finding the other way, a healthier, more empowered way to feel good, so they can do the same. That's when we can expect them to reach their true potential, and that's when they will.

Debbie

Debbie, a young adult no longer in school or working, came to see me months after being in a psychiatric hospital for attempting suicide. She had hit her limit after years of suffering from a chronic medical condition that required multiple surgeries and post-operative care that was cumbersome, intrusive, and humiliating. Such care included having to sleep with an oxygen mask in order to regulate her breath. Debbie explained that each time she went under anesthesia, she wondered if she would ever wake up again. As a result of these experiences, she avoided sleep, and her sleep deprivation made it impossible for her to function well in any context. Doctors had Debbie on Risperdal, Xanax, and Zoloft.

Within moments of meeting Debbie, I taught her 60 Seconds by leading her through the experience, as I do with everyone. Immediately, I could see the outward physiological signs that her roaring amygdala began to calm. Being as sleep-deprived as she was, she actually fell asleep. The tools moved her out of the rev—the "ten" of a racing nervous system—and into the calm, which she had never experienced as anything other than "zero"—the complete shut down of the brain-body into sleep. As Debbie slept, I noticed, to my alarm, that her heart rate soared and pounded aggressively and visibly through her neck. To my amazement, Debbie woke up startled every 40 to 45 seconds. While awake, for no more than a few seconds at a time, she would look around as though she was checking to make sure she was still alive and that everything was okay. I guided her through 60 Seconds each time she woke, having her notice the support of the pillow under her head, for example, until very quickly, she would fall back asleep— for another 40 to 45 seconds only. Debbie would then wake in a startle and check to see if everything was still okay.

The next time I saw Debbie, we continued the use of 60 Seconds, and though she did not fall asleep, she said she felt as though she might. She was able to stay awake in a greater state of ease. This was "the new experience." She was deeply relaxed yet awake, neither "ten" nor "zero." During the next session, we decided we would conduct another "sleep study" to track the quality of her sleep now that she had started using 60 Seconds in her daily life. When she fell asleep this time, she slept peacefully. Her heart rate was regular. There were no outward signs of pounding at all. She did not wake up to check for anything, not one time! Because she told me it was important to her to get off her medications, I let her know this was a good time to begin slowly weaning them, as she continued to use 60 Seconds as often as possible.

Soon enough, Debbie's doctors were surprised by the dramatic, healthy reduction in her blood pressure (numbers they hadn't seen for her in years), as well as her capacity to function well enough without the cocktail of medications she had been on before she started 60 Seconds. Even Debbie was surprised to be off her meds without becoming depressed. Her pulmonary specialist called to ask if I would work with another of his patients.

Katlyn

Katlyn, a young adult, was on her 38th day in hospital for a flare up of her chronic Cystic Fibrosis. She had great difficulty breathing, which caused panic attacks that exacerbated her condition, leading to bronchitis and other complications. Upon the pulmonary specialist's recommendation, the family hired me to see Katlyn in hospital to teach her 60 Seconds. The first time I got to the hospital, Katlyn was having a panic attack and medical providers were hovering around her bed trying to calm her. The family asked everyone to leave so I could work with her and while her father observed, 60 Seconds brought Katlyn out of her panic attack within seconds. After our work was done, her father reported to Katlyn's mother how amazed he was that Katlyn was able to come out of the panic so quickly, remain calm so long, and not cough incessantly as she had been for weeks.

Each time I met with Katlyn she appeared stronger, more alert, more confident, even moving out of the bed to a chair to do our work together. When her mother joined us for our fourth and last meeting together, she said at the end that she felt like she had "just had a massage." These are words I hear from many after experiencing 60 Seconds for as long as twenty minutes or more. With Katlyn, it took four one-hour sessions of deepening the neural pathways for 60 Seconds before she was back at home enjoying her life, living without panic, breathing normally.

When we want to calm down, it's not enough to say, "Take a deep breath." We have to know *how*. Runners, for example, know that a cramp is often the result of breathing shallowly in through the mouth, allowing air into the lungs only, causing a sympathetic response of constriction. Ouch! Short, shallow, rapid breath in through the mouth that only fills the lungs doesn't feel good, and it doesn't help our body function at its best. Talk about bad breath! In fact, let's consider Bad Breath as our nemesis. We don't like it when he's around, signaling to the brain a fight-flight-freeze response that leads to greater constriction.

To rid ourselves of the effects of Bad Breath, runners, for example, know to breathe deeply in through the nose and into the belly in order to release the cramp. Breathing in this way oxygenates the body, thus supporting expansion, openness, and peak performance. Now that's what I call Superbreath! Superbreath comes to our rescue when we breathe deeply in through the nose, filling our entire belly with air. This most life-affirming breath, cape and all, goes deep into the belly to "tickle" the nerve endings that line the stomach, causing a parasympathetic response. The result is greater calm. Thank you, Superbreath!

If we want more internal balance, we need to trigger the parasympathetic *constantly*. Good thing breathing is constant! We breathe how many times in a minute? If we can change the way we're breathing, then every minute of every hour of every day we have the ability to trigger that soothing parasympathetic response. After 21-28 times, Superbreath becomes more automatic. Then, before we know it, all those things that used to be so upsetting aren't as agitating. We may not know exactly why, but we can feel a subtle difference. Our new way of breathing is regulating us from the inside.

Remember, if this calmer response isn't automatic for us yet, it will be. While the neural pathways are forming, don't be discouraged. The more we practice, the stronger they will become until they're deeply embedded in our brain structure. When we work for our tools, our tools work for us. So let's hang in there. We're already halfway through our toolkit! If we're feeling slight improvement, but not drastic change, that's perfect. An incremental transformation of the nervous system is what we're going for here because it indicates we're affecting change at a deep physiological level.

Let's recall Luke now, our X-box player from Chapter One, so we don't give up on this potentially life-changing toolkit. He is a great example of someone who experienced the benefits of 60 Seconds, but wasn't able to feel its effects automatically because he didn't practice. When Luke plays the X-box, he is distracted from what he calls, "a constant buzzing with so many thoughts, I rarely have peace." While playing, he doesn't have to think about, or feel, what it's like to not have a father in his life, or to have a mother who's gone 12 hours a day and exhausted when she gets home. Though Luke knows that 60 Seconds brings him out of a near constant sleepy state to a more alert presence, making him better able to focus, it has not yet become a quicker fix than the X-box. In order for the benefits of 60 Seconds to kick in automatically, he has to initiate the experience at least 21-28 times.

Changing our habits comes down to really wanting the change, and wanting to experience our self and our life differently. (It helps to be fed up with not having the life we want!)

Having said that, it's okay to be in the place in between. Some of us may find ourselves going through multiple experiences of contrast: learning this new way of finding peace, while returning to old habits despite greater, negative consequences. Going back and forth for a while, maybe for a long while, between using 60 Seconds, feeling its relief, and continuing to use our drug of choice is okay. Our brain-body will experience the contrast of that—feeling some relief *with* side effects using our drug of choice, and feeling relief *without* side effects using 60 Seconds. These contrasting experiences help us get clearer about what we really want. With time and practice, we begin to notice that 60 Seconds indeed brings relief quickly— and it does so without making our life more difficult or unhealthy.

Even more fun than that is when, inevitably, we begin to notice 60 Seconds kicking in even when we aren't *deliberately* practicing it! This is the automaticity I was talking about that occurs when the rehearsal becomes rote. Once we've stuck with the tools long enough, we begin to *automatically* breathe in through our nose and deep into our belly more often than not. We begin to *automatically* notice that we are connected to solid ground that helps us feel more secure. We begin to *automatically* notice the support available to us in each moment. When all this begins to happen more unconsciously because it has been hardwired through repetitive experience, 60 Seconds becomes a much more viable alternative to self-medication or any other form of coping.

We may start to find ourselves noticing, *Hey! I'm feeling better more often than I used to. Maybe this stuff is working. Maybe I'll do 60 Seconds more often. I could even try sitting here and using my tools before pouring this glass of wine. Maybe doing 60 Seconds will help me savor this glass of wine longer. Maybe I won't end up pouring a second or third glass. Maybe I can really enjoy the wine for the experience rather than the escape.*

60 seconds is a process, rather than a Eureka! A-ha! Moment. It very subtly rewires the brain through experience. However, subtle doesn't mean slow! The changes actually happen far quicker than we think and are far more rewarding than we imagine—we just have to notice them. Breathing in through our nose and deep into the belly slows our nervous system enough for us to become aware of the profound and lasting impact we are creating in our nervous system, priming us to live less hectic, more stable and joyful lives.

For Debbie and Katlyn, learning how to breathe in the most optimum way greatly improved their capacity to tolerate the multiple challenges they faced while living with a serious medical condition. Their peace of mind and body were tested constantly. Out of a dark sense of hopelessness, they began to feel enormous power.

Playtime

Right now, I invite you to notice each of the tools we have reviewed so far: first, feel your feet on the ground, wiggling your toes, imagining your roots, perhaps. Then, notice the support of whatever you are sitting in, give into that support, and allow the support to do all the work. Try giving all the places in your body that are working too hard permission to rest. Now shift your awareness to your breath. Breathe in through your nose and try imagining the air whooshing into your belly, blowing it up like a balloon. Feel your diaphragm muscles expand as the air travels all the way down. Watch your belly rise as it fills with oxygen. (If it's not rising, it's okay. Just breathe in through your nose and shift your focus back to your feet on the ground, then the support of what you're in, the chair, bed, couch, or wherever you are.)

Now find your anchor, the part of you that feels the most solidly planted inside or weighted down. As you begin to take note of what is happening inside your body, become aware of the relief, however slight at first. It may be a dropping, settling, expanding, opening up, loosening, tingling, or warming sensation. You'll get better over time at noticing when you are moving out of sympathetic into parasympathetic, out of "zero-ten-ing" and into The Zone. When you focus on that shift, it often increases. Once you have done this for 60 seconds, you may find yourself wanting to sit in the experience longer, which I welcome you to do, and if not, that's great too. This is all just a beginning and meant to develop over time with ease.

This week, become curious about which one of the tools you've learned so far is the easiest for you to access. While driving in the car, for example, notice if you begin to feel a sense of urgency and impatience with yourself, with traffic, or with the other drivers around you. You may find yourself bracing more, getting tighter, or gripping the steering wheel as you navigate the roads to reach your destination. Try using that physical tension as a cue to use the tools you are currently learning, starting with the one that comes to your mind the easiest. Perhaps, you can begin by taking in a deep breath, in through your nose to fill your belly with air. If so, simply focus on your breath for a moment. If that particular tool isn't easily accessible, try feeling your left foot planted on the floor of the car (your right foot is working the pedals) as well as the support of the car seat on your back. Notice your butt planted in the car seat as your anchor, and focus some attention there to feel how solid and connected it is. You may find that using your tools while driving helps you feel a little less tense and a little less urgent. When you do, you can begin to entertain new thoughts of greater ease like, "I'll get there when I get there, and everything will be fine."

5
Tool Four:
See It To Be It

Every picture, whether real or imagined, has an effect on our physiological state, and our physiological state is what determines how well we do no matter our endeavor. In other words, **seeing affects being,** so we better be selective about the pictures we allow ourselves to see! Visualization does much to keep us in or out of The Zone.

We can't exactly control our dreams, but if you've ever had a vivid dream, you have likely noticed that the dream seemed so real to you, that part of you believed, even though you knew it was just a dream, that it must have actually happened. That's because neurons fire in our brain when we see images that trick the brain into believing we are having the experience. In fact, if, while dreaming, we were hooked up to the kinds of mechanics that gauge our brain activity as well as our physiology, such as heart rate and blood pressure, we would see that our brain-body goes through a chain of physiological events identical to the ones we would have if we were having the experience in reality.

As part of the program I created for schools called *Brain Charge*, I recommend that teachers, administrators, and support staff utilize visualization to help keep students in The Zone. When we are in The Zone of optimum physiological arousal, with just enough anxiety to pique our interest and enlist our grit, we get things done. For this reason, I suggest hanging large pictures of nature in the rooms where students will be. This way, they can help themselves feel good by looking at what is automatically soothing to the brain-body. If we can't actually be in nature, we can see it in a picture or in our mind, and immediately begin to feel the same effects as the actual experience. Some people may be triggered negatively by a water scene or dense forest, so it is good to have different options to choose from. Each of us is hardwired to thrive, so each of us will naturally gravitate towards the particular image that makes us feel best. Notice the images you keep around you. Observe how they make you feel inside when you look at them. Be sure to surround yourself with what helps you feel your best.

Imagining success is a visual that helps us feel good. Seeing the outcome we want in our mind's eye pumps up the brain-body with a particular combination of neurochemicals (serotonin, endorphins, and dopamine) that fuel our strength and power, creating the foundation for our belief that we can do it. Visualizing ourselves engaged in the process from the very beginning to the end strengthens our capacity for success, especially when we can see ourselves enacting every step along the way.

A now well-reported study of basketball players illustrates the invaluable benefit of visualization for success.[11] There were three groups in the experiment: One group of players was told to go to the free-throw line on a basketball court and practice free-throw shots for 30 minutes. Another group was told to do nothing. This was the control group. A third group of players was told NOT to go onto a basketball court or hold a basketball, but instructed to see for 30 minutes, in their mind's eye, sinking their free-throw shots. At the end of the practice period, there was no difference in performance between the group of players who actually practiced—on the court, sweating, exerting, and strengthening their muscles through physical action—and those who only imagined themselves shooting successfully. Both groups performed equally well and better than the control group.

This study, as well as the many others that have replicated these findings, has been instrumental in changing the way we understand the workings of the brain, and what kinds of therapies and interventions work best, no matter what the issue—performance anxiety, underachievement, or victimization. When we envision ourselves as powerfully performing in the way we want, we exercise our brain. We grow the brain's neural pathways for the possibility of creating that very performance in reality. When we go to perform the way we want in real life after having imagined it over and over again, our brain says, *Hey, I've done this before, I know how to do this*, and our muscles and mind engage in the behavior as though they already have.

Visualization is one of the five tools of 60 Seconds because of how powerfully it can rewire the brain for greater success. Visualizing being securely rooted to the earth, for example, helps us feel more grounded when we can't quickly feel our feet on the ground through the channel of sensation. Most of us, during times of stress, whether or not we're aware, cannot feel our feet on the ground. Debbie, for example, from her significant history of trauma, could not feel her feet on the ground when we first started working together. Through visualization of roots growing out from the bottom of her feet, spreading in every direction, and connecting deeply into the center of Mother Earth, Debbie was able to feel the physical sensation of her feet planted on solid ground. Visualization increased her awareness of feeling grounded over time. Soon, Debbie was coming into the office and all the tools of 60 Seconds were having their grounding effect instantaneously.

Just like Debbie, we're getting there! We're now learning the fourth tool of 60 Seconds and seeing the importance of practice. Remember, the more we practice these tools, the more automatic they become and the quicker we feel their effects. Soon enough, practice turns into habit.

Several sessions into our work together, I asked Debbie right at the top of the hour to become aware of which of her tools she was able to notice first. Without pause, she said the support of the couch on her back, and her feet on solid ground, in that order. I asked her to focus on the physical experience she was having with those two tools and to tell me what else she noticed. She said, "My butt's my anchor." Just like an anchor plunges down to the bottom of the ocean's floor with the weight of gravity, we too have gravity working in us. There are parts of our body when we are standing that feel more anchored than other parts, because the weight of our body rests there—on our feet, for example. When we are sitting, we have parts of our body that feel more anchored than others, like our bottom, again because of gravity doing its job. Gravity is at work whether or not we notice it, but when we do notice it, and use imagery of an actual anchor doing its job, we find that somewhere inside us we feel more anchored to what we are in or on. This gives us a sense of security and stability.

When I asked Debbie what else she was noticing, she replied simply with, "Nothing." She was using her tools to have a sensory experience in the present moment without anything else in her awareness. No thoughts, no pains, no urgency, no stories, no criticisms, no to-do lists, no fears, nothing. I asked Debbie what the nothingness was saying, and she sat with the question for a moment before she replied, "That nothing's wrong."

Wow. We celebrated that for a while, sitting in it, enjoying it, allowing for the neural pathways of that experience to deepen in her brain-body so she could get to that state more automatically in the future. After a few words about the experience she was presently having and what it could mean for her life, we went back to the conscious use of the tools. When she focused on them again I asked her what she noticed this time. "Nothing again," she said with a smile and a little laugh. This was exciting because she got there again, back to the state of nothingness that told her nothing is wrong, this time quicker and easier because her neural pathways were strengthening with each mindful use of the tools. I asked her what the nothingness was like this time and it took her a while to speak the word that came to her mind because, as she explained, she didn't understand it. She had never used the word before and didn't know its meaning. The word rose out of the physiological state she was in, the bottom-up experience. She said, "Stoic."

We looked the word up to be sure of its richest, fullest meaning and learned that it is used to describe a "calm acceptance of all occurrences as the unavoidable result of divine will or of the natural order." Wow again. Goosebumps! We were both in awe.

When Debbie came in the next time, she looked even healthier, and was clearly more energized. She smiled more and showed a clear sense of excitement. When she began grounding her effervescence with 60 Seconds, she noticed that she was feeling excitement without fear, something she told me she hadn't been able to feel for a long time. Since her suicide attempt and hospitalization months earlier, anytime she would feel activation in her nervous system, it would scare her, even if that activation came in the form of joy. The physical experience of joyful excitement was associated with fear and stress. At the root of each of these emotions is the same elevation in physiology, an activation of the nervous system. But now, in a grounded way, Debbie was experiencing her excitement without fear. What was that like for her, I asked, and she said, "happy." I wanted her to notice that specific feeling in her body, name it, and be in it.

Soon, Debbie shifted out of "sinking" into the couch for its support. Her excitement propelled her forward. Because I always listen to and follow the impulses of the body, I asked Debbie to stand. She jumped up willingly, when in previous sessions she had found it too tiring to stand for exercises. She noticed this time, and exclaimed with joy, "I'm not tired!" Her excitement was grounded. It was not draining her in the way stress can drain. She described feeling, "Rooted." I asked her to focus on that feeling and to notice what else was happening inside. Debbie came up with another word neither one of us was sure of, "Sedimentary." When we looked it up it meant, "Consolidation of broken fragments." We both knew how huge this was for her. She was feeling consolidated. The multiple surgeries she had had over many years, and all the stress, terror, and trauma that went along with those experiences, left Debbie feeling fragmented as a person, beyond unstable and insecure. Using 60 Seconds allowed Debbie to connect with resources inside of her that restored a sense of integration, a sense of strength, power, and peace.

I taught Debbie another visualization that I teach to everyone with whom I work. I learned it from my colleague who calls it the "container." The container is an imagined construct that is unique to each one of us; it is ours and ours alone. It completely surrounds and protects us with a force field of strength. Seeing our container in our mind's eye allows us to connect more deeply with our own healthy boundaries in order to strengthen them. Having limits and knowing them, noticing them, and speaking up about them, serves to protect us from overwhelm. Having a visual image of our container's physicality to go along with our sense of such limits is highly effective.

Each one of us requires a certain amount of personal space, for example. Boundaries help to define how much personal space we need in order to feel comfortable and safe. Some of us need more personal space than others but we all need to feel like our permission is required for others to enter it. When our boundaries get broken down due to excessive stress or trauma, and we allow people to "walk all over us" or "take up all the space" available in the room, physically or energetically, our brain-body gets worn down and fed up, even if we try telling ourselves that it's all okay. You know what I'm talking about, all you martyrs and overachievers out there! ☺

When we are disconnected from a clear sense of our own personal space with its limits and boundaries, we are ineffective at saying "no" and meaning it. We don't embody the "no," which leads to people not hearing our "no," even when we muster up enough courage to speak it. The fear of confrontation we have about saying "no" often leads to passive-aggressive or other unwanted behavior. This is when we tell our loved ones "yes" to their face and later act on the "no" we wish we could have said in the first place. Our true "no," the one we could have said in the moment if we had healthy boundaries, is so much more civilized than some of the passive-aggressive stunts we pull out of resentment. Who wants to keep living like that? It's not fun. It's not good for our kids, and it's not good for us.

When we visualize our container and feel ourselves grounded and anchored inside of it, we begin to feel a sense of safety that allows us to expand into more of who we really are. The imagined force field around our container protects us from other people's stories, expectations, and scripts. Other people and their stuff don't get into our container without our permission. Envisioning ourselves over and over again anchored inside our protective container allows us to live as big as we want, being all of who we are. This is how we get clearer about how we want to feel, and how we want to live.

For some of us, this may be sounding really new. Exciting, isn't it? As we envision ourselves being the way we want to be, we get to feel the way we want to feel. When we have this experience in our imagination first, it becomes far more likely in reality. This helps us get clearer, and therefore more capable of articulating our wants and needs more directly, gently but firmly so that people understand we mean business.

When we are honest and authentic, it gives everyone around us permission to be the same—our partners, our children, and everyone else we say we love. We start acting in ways that are consistent with what we say we want because we've aligned our brain-body with our aspirations. Imagining ourselves being fully truthful and authentic and basking in those good feelings make it impossible for us to live any other way on any other day. Operating on this level of truth heals and creates, inspires and excites—us first, then our children. What a lasting contribution to the planet.

My container is a canopy of trees in a forest. I stand as a Sequoia tree firmly rooted to Mother Earth, and I can feel all the other trees protecting me, standing firmly, blocking out with their branches and leaves everything and everyone. Inside my container I get to stand erect with the confidence I have to operate from my truth no matter what others think of it. I am whole and separate inside my container. I don't feel separated from my son or anyone else. Separation is a different feeling from separateness. Separation is when we feel disconnected from others. *Separateness*, something entirely different, allows for each of us to be individually whole and complete on our own *while* connecting with others when we choose. When I feel whole and separate in my container, I give permission to my son and everyone else to feel whole and separate in their container. From that place, we get to choose to connect and join in healthy ways for the purpose of true intimacy and joy.

Curtis' container is his Jacuzzi with the water so hot and the air so cold that massive amounts of steam hover all around him. The steam provides complete coverage as a visible force field keeps everybody and everything else outside the steam as well as the boundaries of the Jacuzzi. I have clients, students, friends, and family members with every container you can think of, from cars and army tanks to spaceships, from perfume bottles and hearts to glass houses. My son recently informed me during some rough-housing with friends, when I asked him if he was okay at the bottom of the pile of the kids he was under, he popped out his head and said, "Don't worry, Mom. I'm in my box."

When he was three and four, he used to leave the house to go to school in his "white light." He's eight now, and his light has morphed into a box all on its own. We recently did 60 Seconds, at his insistence, and his box became golden. When once we had to consciously focus on the building up of his tools to curb his instinct to hit others when provoked, I see now that his tools are in him working automatically, allowing him far more restraint because of the natural self-regulation the tools created in his nervous system.

I have also used visualization to heal myself both from feelings of unworthiness as well as beliefs that I was unlovable because of how I was treated growing up. One year in particular, when I was working as a psychologist in the public schools, I drove to work each day at the same time, and a song would come on the radio. It was *True Colors*, originally performed by Cyndi Lauper, but performed in this case by Phil Collins. It occurred to me one day to hear my mother singing the words of that song to me. Each time it came on the radio, whether I was already in front of the school or not, I stayed in the car long enough to hear the whole song, imagining my mother singing me the words from a very real and deep place in her heart. I knew she would probably never be able to say anything like that to me in reality, but I knew that imagining her as a healthy person capable of speaking those words if she could—and meaning them—would go a long way towards giving me the feelings inside my brain-body I needed in order to heal.

It worked. In reality, I have to keep my conversations with my mother short and sweet, few and far between, though I love her very much. My visualization of how I wish things could be is not how our conversations go. They don't give me the feeling the song gives me, but that's okay. I imagine my mom the way I need her to be, and I keep myself from the reality of her as much as I can. This way, I can go on giving my brain-body the better feelings it needs in order for me to live my life well. In turn, I am better able to give my son what he needs. Some people would judge this negatively as avoidance of reality. They might even call it selfish. I'm so grateful to have the neuroscience behind me now, so I can say with much joy, "Rubbish!"

I believe each one of us would gladly be the person who could sing those words and mean them to everyone we love, if we weren't so affected by the stress of life. With 60 Seconds, we have at our disposal tools to offset the pressure, so we can be more of the person we want to be and enjoy a greater sense of power and self-control. Governance over ourselves: isn't that what we want? What could be bigger than that? As some of my clients tell me, even when they don't feel like using the tools, they get an immediate "hit" of relief from remembering they have them, and that they work.

The power of knowing how to create lasting change in our life is an essential feeling to have. It fuels us. It is lost when we are traumatized or under so much stress that we feel out of control of our reactions. Feeling powerless is at the root of what people call low self-esteem. Low self-esteem is a psychological term. Powerlessness is a physiological state. It is the depletion in the brain-body of all the important neurochemistry that feeds our sense of strength and capacity. The only way to feel powerful is to have *experiences* of being powerful. This isn't always easy in reality. But it is possible through visualization. When we imagine ourselves setting out to do something and in our mind's eye we do it, a neurochemical concoction surges through our blood from the brain that gives us a palpable feeling of being strong, powerful, and capable. This neurochemical reaction happens even though we are imagining the experience and not actually having it. When we visualize our success and power enough times, including all the details of it, sitting in the physical sensations and feelings that the visualization brings, we build neural pathways that fuel our capacity to be that powerful person for real.

Getting grounded, feeling supported, finding our anchor, envisioning our container protecting us, and knowing how to breathe so that every breath fills us with a greater sense of strength and self-control - *that* is how we offset stress and lower the cortisol it sends through the brain-body. Noticing when we need to calm down is one thing. Combining that awareness with actually knowing *how* to calm down, without needing to resort to something with side effects? That's true power! Notice your internal, natural power now as you use the tools we've learned so far. The next chapter will explain more about why I am always guiding us to notice, or to become more aware of what we are noticing.

Playtime

Right now, sit somewhere comfortable and put your feet flat on the ground. If it's difficult to feel the sensation of your feet solidly planted, simply wiggle your toes, push your heels into the ground, or imagine roots growing out from the bottom of your soles into Mother Earth. If you prefer, in your mind's eye, imagine standing down at the tide of the beach sinking a little into wet sand.

Breathe in through your nose, filling your belly with air, as you notice the support of whatever you are sitting in. Scan your body and notice where it feels like it's beginning to sink in or become more weighted down. Find your anchor—the part of you that is most solidly planted in whatever you are sitting in. Focus on the pleasant sensations of your anchor.

As you feel more rooted, weighted, planted, and grounded, allow your container to come into view. See yourself anchored inside the container that protects you from everyone and everything that is not you. What does your container look like? See its size, shape, and color. Spend as much time as you want basking in it. Feel a force field around it that disallows others to enter without your permission. Have this important dual focus for a moment: you are both anchored and contained.

Notice the sensations and feelings you have as you get to be in your own personal space connecting to who you really are without the noise, expectation, stories, beliefs, judgments, criticisms, and values of anyone else. See yourself free and whole inside your container being exactly who you want to be, feeling exactly how you want to feel. If feeling the bigness and separateness of you is a new or foreign feeling, consider this: your imagination is a safe way to explore the possibility of having healthy boundaries, even with the people you love the most.

This week, try to notice the *very first* annoyance or hassle that begins to rev your physiology upward, perhaps moving you out of The Zone. It may be first thing in the morning, when you wake up and see that you are already running behind schedule. That very first moment when the stress response is triggered is when we want to become more aware. Now that we've been learning and practicing our tools for a while, our neural pathways are strengthening in a very healthy way, and we may be able to use our tools at the earliest provocation of stress; the earlier, the better. You may get into the car to drive to work, for example, and see that you don't have enough gas in the tank to make it. Perhaps you make the stop to fill the tank but the gas pump doesn't work properly, slowing you down further. Whichever the *first* annoyance is, see if you can temper its physiological effects with whatever tool from 60 Seconds comes to you the easiest. Once you have your first tool working for you, see if you can add one or two more.

And thank yourself, please, for choosing to experience a new way of transcending stress right in the first moment of noticing it. By actively calming, rather than ignoring stress, letting it build until you grab a less healthy fix, immediate self-soothing with 60 Seconds pays off exponentially in the long run—not just for you and your health, but also for everyone around you. There's no need to check out when you can feel good checking *in* quickly.

6
Tool Five:
Noticing

One of my teachers once said that the definition of mental health is "the ability to observe one's own behavior." That was a light bulb moment for me at the time. I knew if I could notice the impact my behavior was having on another person or situation, *and if I could adjust my behavior accordingly*, then I would probably experience more peace. Not surprisingly, peace eluded me. You could have played reels upon reels of my behavior back to me on a movie screen and I wouldn't have claimed it as my own. Even when I was screaming at the top of my lungs spewing expletives, I wasn't aware that others experienced that as anger. *Coo-coo*, I know, but at the time, I thought I was sad. I was hurt. Those were the feelings I connected to. Angry? Not me.

We have since learned that the ability to be "the observer" of your own body's responses is essential not only to mental health but also to physical health and beyond. The observing or "noticing" we do with 60 Seconds has long been recognized as "sensory awareness" – the capacity to feel the sensations of the body *and* be aware of them at the same time. *What sensations am I noticing now? Am I warm, hot, cold, hungry, achy, tired, restless, racy, jittery, calm, tense, tight, loose, relaxed, heavy, light?* It turns out that being able to answer that question is at the root of much success in life: behaviorally with preventing antisocial behavior, interpersonally with the development of empathy, psychologically with getting well in psychotherapy, and academically with learning how to read.

Reading programs that incorporate an element of sensory awareness work well for anyone who has struggled to learn how to read. The Lindamood-Bell Reading Program has students stand up while they learn, engaging their whole body to activate not just the left brain, but also the right, or more sensory, brain as well.[12] While feeling the weight of their body on their feet, students are instructed to use visualization to imagine the word they are learning - what it looks like, feels like, smells like, and any other images the word elicits. Then, students are instructed to put their hands over their mouths, then on their cheeks, then on their throats, to notice the physical sensations they experience in these different parts of the body when saying letters, letter combinations and words. Students are asked if the sounds made by the words are open, round, tight, or airy. *Does the sound pop? Does it make a vibration? If so, where? When you make the sound does your jaw get tighter or looser?* When we enlist our ability to notice sensations while learning how to read, the right brain works in unison with the left, allowing the whole brain to move along in harmony as an integrated, well-oiled machine.

As far back as the 1970s and 80s, a researcher and practitioner named Eugene Gendlin wanted to understand why when he conducted therapy with many of the same kinds of people—educated, intelligent, verbal, depressed and/or anxious—some would get better and some would not. After controlling for variables of difference, he found that what distinguished between the people who got better with therapy and those who did not was sensory awareness.[13] The people who were able to access not only their thoughts and feelings during therapy, but also their physical sensations, healed more quickly and experienced more long-term positive effects. This is why throughout the book and with each tool, I stress noticing.

The people who get well and stay well are the people who are able to notice, "When I think about this, and it makes me angry, my jaw clenches, my chest gets tight, and I feel an impulse to hit or push." Gendlin found that when he had his subjects focus on the "felt sense" of their experience—the awareness of physical sensations—its intensity and level of discomfort would lessen. His subjects soon felt relief. From a neuroscientific perspective, this is an effective way of working because it includes not only thoughts and feelings in the therapeutic process, but also physical sensations. With this approach, we engage *the whole brain*, which of course is involved in every experience we have. If we want to heal something, we need to allow for the processing of everything—thoughts, feelings, *and* sensations. *Noticing* the physical sensations that accompany our thoughts and feelings integrates all parts of the brain so we can heal and move forward more completely.

When we have a thought, our neocortex or higher order brain lights up and becomes active. When we experience an emotion, like anger, fear, joy, or any other emotion, our mid-brain, also called the limbic brain, lights up. Physical sensations, such as rapid heart rate and tension, light up the brain stem or reptilian brain that revs up to defend the whole brain-body if necessary. These are the three parts of what neuroscientists call the triune brain: the neocortex or thinking brain, the limbic or feeling brain, and the brain stem that processes sensations. When we bring sensations into our awareness in a safe and comfortable way—after we use 60 Seconds for grounding and support, for example—then we are able to notice how they can resolve and release quickly and quietly. When we ignore them, however, we don't get to notice how easily the brain-body can self-regulate. "What goes up must come down."

When done within the context of 60 Seconds, noticing heals. Ignoring postpones. Without tools, ignoring, or what some call avoidance, is helpful because at least we are not focusing on a problem when we have no solution. That makes things worse. Now, however, because we have tools, we don't *need* to ignore as much as we used to. With the physiological benefits of our tools, we now have more options of responses from which to choose. We can use the physical signs of stress as cues to begin focusing NOT on the reaction of the body that's stressed, but on the soothed reaction of the body once our tools kick in, whether automatically or more consciously.

When stress is ignored and left mounting in the brain-body day after day, the amygdala sounds off its alarm incessantly, trying to get us to do something to take care of ourselves. Our heart beats faster. Our blood pressure goes up. We brace, tighten up, and breathe less deeply. We also feel less tolerant, less patient, more urgent and agitated. When we live this way for most of the day, day after day, we get worn down. Every organ becomes taxed by chronic stress, increasing the onset of disease and reducing our lifespan if we don't utilize a healthy antidote.[14]

One part of the brain most affected by the stress response is the hippocampus. This is the part of the brain that consolidates memory and is also functionally linked to the part of the neocortex that keeps our emotions and arousal regulated, the orbitofrontal cortex. Quite simply, when the hippocampus is robust and healthy, it communicates well with the orbitofrontal cortex, supporting us to be less reactive, certainly less *over*reactive. With chronic stress and no use of the antidote, however, the hippocampus loses its essential neural pathways for such communication. It literally shrinks in size and we become far less regulated and more reactive. This is when we become susceptible to a Bandaid, quick fix, or self-medication in an attempt to control and/or numb our feelings.

From years of being both a therapist and client, I believe that the feelings we experience after we've been out of control of our own reactions and behaviors are some of the hardest feelings to tolerate. Not being able to stop ourselves from reacting to certain people and situations, whether we do so overtly through a behavior or we bottle our reaction to fester, we feel such shame and pain, we just want it to end. "Bring on the beer!" is what I'd say, before 60 Seconds, that is.

60 Seconds, with its emphasis on noticing grounding and support, sends powerful messages to the amygdala and brain-body that everything is okay. When we notice the sensations of the body that are pleasant, balanced, and calm, cortisol decreases. Messages of alert are quieted. We rest and restore. The longer we can be in this calmer state *with the awareness that we are in it,* the stronger our neurons for calm fire, the quicker neural pathways for calm form, and the greater our capacity for calm becomes. The amygdala eventually stops firing as strongly or as often. It ultimately goes off unless absolutely required for survival (which is what we want). Peace is restored— or for some, experienced for the first time.

Kelly

Kelly came to see me as a young adult, unable to work or attend college. She shared her long history of being in and out of psychiatric hospitals, eating disorder clinics, and rehabs for drugs and alcohol. She went through a long list of diagnoses and former medications. She came in with active thoughts of not wanting to be alive by the end of the year. Why would she want to live any longer, she thought, when she was unable to drive a car, hold a job, or see friends? She had become afraid of everything. She was paralyzed. Kelly told me that the only reason she decided to give me a chance was because she read about my approach and realized it was the only thing she hadn't yet tried. Was there really one last hope? *Did she* dare *believe in the possibility that she could feel a different way than she had always felt—numb, disconnected, confused, ugly, depressed, anxious, lethargic, hopeless, and paralyzed by fear?*

After several sessions of 60 Seconds, Kelly told me what our first sessions together were like for her. She was completely confused! She didn't understand what we were doing and thought it was strange. She stuck with it only because ever so subtly after each session she began noticing *that she was feeling more relief. She didn't comprehend how that was possible from something as simple as feeling her feet on the ground, and noticing support, breath, and containment, but it was undeniable to her that she was beginning to feel better than she had felt in many years. While she was visualizing her container one time – for her, a cloud that was protected by an "orb," within which she could feel herself getting "recharged"—Kelly was astounded by the new experience she was having of herself. She quietly said, "This is what other people mean when they use the word peace." The more she sat in the peace with awareness, the more she was able to get back to it in less time and with greater ease.*

Kelly came into my office one time to report that she was able to walk by someone on the sidewalk without any anxiety at all. When once she would have had to cross to the other side of the street or find some other way to avoid being close to a stranger, she now felt no sensations of fear, trepidation, terror, or any of the other feelings she once had. None. She simply walked on by and noticed afterwards what she had done. It was a nonevent, when once she would have become instantaneously hypervigilant from the presence of another. Kelly was so excited to tell me about her new experience. She knew it was a big sign that whatever we were doing was working.

Within six months of fairly regular weekly sessions that included some talking and some 60 Seconds, Kelly was driving, had a full-time job, and was seeing friends. She started running every day and taking a photography class, and perhaps most importantly, her thoughts of ending her life were at bay. She finally had hope and was beginning to believe in a future.

When we can feel peace in our body and be fully aware and focused on the relief, the calm, and the flow that it gives us, we want not only to live, but also to live with greater connection to who we really are and to who our loved ones really are. Better still, we do so with more passion as professionals and parents. On the other hand, when our amygdala is causing physical sensations of such discomfort that we can't stand feeling our own body, or hearing our own mind, we don't want to be connected more deeply to ourselves, our children, or anyone else. No way! It is only when we feel relief from all of that, that we can live, really live, as the people we want to be.

Relief from discomfort and pain allows us to experience freedom from a racing, analyzing, judging, criticizing, fearing, doubting, worrying mind. Yay! And when we feel that relief *not* from a pill or another way of numbing, we feel our power. (See the cape flowing from your back, Super Human!) Feeling our power, however slightly, time after time, with awareness, restores hope and possibility. When we become *aware* and we practice *noticing,* we realize that in just seconds these tools calm and quiet our mind. When it does, we have that magic combination of few thoughts, if any, and a physical state of peace in our body. Now we can choose. We have more options. We don't need to eat or shop as much or as often, or engage in any other kind of addictive or harmful behavior that keeps us from feeling ourselves and connecting to our loved ones. We have tools that are medically proven and scientifically supported to quickly release in our brain the same "feel good" stuff released by a good glass of red wine.

Not only does 60 Seconds release GABA, an important neurotransmitter that elicits in the brain-body a greater state of calm quickly, but it also has other biochemical benefits. 60 Seconds releases serotonin, endorphins, and dopamine; it lowers cortisol, heart rate, and blood pressure. It is the pill without the side effects, the drink you can have and still drive, the joint that doesn't put a fog between you and your kids. It is the "answer" my beer buzz was at age 13, but without the dreaded yet inevitable "walk of shame" that followed. Instead, we get to have relief quickly *and* be more present wherever we go, whoever we're with – it's *in* us!

Playtime

Right now, let's deepen our capacity for sensory awareness. Let's notice that when we feel our feet flat on the ground, when we take in the support of what we are sitting in, when we breathe in through our nose and we visualize ourselves as anchored inside our protective container, we feel relief. Let's practice *noticing* in order to strengthen those neural pathways, and observe that even if there is some discomfort inside, if we focus instead on our tools, the discomfort begins to lessen. Our negative and invading thoughts begin to fade, and we feel more comfortable. You can do this for 60 seconds at a time, or less. Five seconds of just noticing your feet on the ground, ten seconds of noticing your breath in through your nose, or 30 seconds of support from your chair are all great. No matter what kind of time you spend on the tools, if you use them repeatedly, over time you can't help but build neural pathways for greater sensory awareness, self-regulation, and joy.

This week, practice your new tool of *noticing* the times when you are talking more than you need to be. Perhaps you are over-explaining something you could say in fewer words or you are defending yourself to someone who doesn't really matter. Perhaps you are over-correcting your child or venting to a friend about something you would feel better not talking about at all. Many times, in challenging situations, it would serve us much better to stop talking, or at least say less. All we need to learn how to do, in order to make this different response possible, is calm the uncomfortable feelings inside our body that drive the excessive talking. That's where 60 Seconds comes in. Whichever tool in the toolkit comes to you the easiest is the perfect place to start. Once you get a little relief from that, then simply add one or two more tools for even more relief in those moments when fewer words are the ticket.

Finally, observe what great work you have done for yourself and those who get to be around you in this new way. You are creating subtle yet profound changes in your life that happen to matter to a whole lot of people.

7
Why Fakin' It Ain't Makin' It

We did it! We learned all five tools of our toolkit, 60 Seconds. By now, we have likely realized why I call the book, *The 60 Seconds Fix* – because it takes just 60 seconds to feel the effects of the tools working together for a safer, healthier fix than the ones we may be used to. As we know, all we need to do to feel those effects more automatically in our everyday life is to practice. How great is it that we can simply practice during moments like showering, driving, standing in line, or sitting at our computer looking something up? In fact, one of my favorite times to seize an opportunity for soothing is when I Bing, rather than Google. Each time I go to Bing's homepage, there it is: a truly awesome picture, usually of nature, that cues me to take a deep breath in through my nose, feel my feet on the ground, and notice my bottom anchored in my seat. (And no, Bing isn't paying me any money to say this! ☺) Whichever of the tools we can use in any naturally occurring moment is just perfect, and that's all it takes to begin living a life that feels more real.

Let me talk to you about fakin' it: Those of us who are partnered up in relationships or those of us who are parents, you'll probably know what I'm talking about. We would love to be able to fake it 'til we make it, wouldn't we? Our partners or kids feel our tension and ask us what's wrong, and we automatically say, "Nothing," when in fact, there may be a whole lot wrong. We're stressed, sometimes scared, angry, resentful, beyond exhausted, sore, in pain, miserable, not really wanting to live another day, not like this, and it all shows in our body no matter what words come out of our mouth.

A friend recently told me that her partner needs an hour to recover after the morning routine of getting their daughter off to school. He finds it so stressful to be around them in the morning that after it's finally over, he retreats to a quiet room to center and ground himself before he can start his workday. My friend was baffled when he told her this. She said, "I don't *talk* like I'm stressed. In fact, the opposite: I try really hard to talk quietly and calmly. I don't get it." Essentially, what she's wondering is why her fakin' it ain't makin' it: *I know my blood is boiling on the inside from the stress of this chaotic morning routine, but I'm not showing it. I'm talking calmly and quietly and doing everything else I can to make it look like I'm fine.* The truth is that the people around us *feel* the truth. We *sense* how someone else *really* feels regardless of how great he or she is at acting.

One of my favorite stories comes from a high school teacher in the Midwest who stood up to address the whole audience at one of my educational seminars. She was excited to learn the science behind why she had a particular experience with a student.

She wanted us to know what happened when a student stopped her in the hall one day.

"I see what you do every time you see me in the hall, Miss," he said to her. "I see you smiling at everyone else until you get to me. As soon as you see me, you stop smiling."

Oh my God. I'm so busted, she thought. *What do I do?* She knew he was right. This was a student at the school she didn't particularly love, let alone like, and here she was being confronted about it. He went on to ask for what he wanted, as many of the children in our lives do.

"Do me a favor," he said. "From now on, when you see me, would you please smile at me more?"

There it was. The request. We get asked all the time—from people young and old, close or distant. There are people in our life who make it clear what they need from us in order to feel better, to maintain connection, and to stay in relationship. Some of us have the self-regulatory capacity to look at ourselves, dig deep, and make the effort, and some of us don't. Some of us, for good reason, are stuck in a nervous system and brain-body that is as tight and revved as a pulled elastic band, ready to snap at anyone who dares to make one more request.

This teacher had a simple choice: to smile more when she saw him or not smile more when she saw him. She could have rationalized why this confrontation and request was ridiculous. She could have defended herself and denied his reality and experience. She could have gone on to ignore and avoid him so that she wouldn't have to comply or give in to the request. Instead, she chose to give it a try. She started walking down the hall *looking for him!* She wasn't going to let him catch her NOT smiling at him one more time. When she saw him the next time, she saw him first—mission accomplished—and flashed him a smile. *Ha! Ha! I did it!* She thought, *He can't get me now.*

He stopped her again and said, "That was so fake!" (Poor girl. I wanted to give her a big hug for trying.)

The science this teacher learned at my seminar that explained this experience is the following: we are all hardwired from birth to do whatever it takes to get relief and feel better, whatever that may be. As newborns, we protest with our cries and demand that we are fed, burped, and put to bed. As we get older, we let people know what we need with either a direct statement or a behavior that communicates less directly. Our protests as adolescents and adults can get as loud as an infant screaming for a diaper change. *Do something, please! I feel gross!* Only when we feel better does the amygdala calm down to communicate an essential message to the brain-body: we are going to be okay. Life will go on, and things will get better. And so somehow, in some way, directly or otherwise, we all end up asking for what we need.

The newly-smiling teacher learned that when we smile, it lowers heart rate, blood pressure, and cortisol levels, in both the person smiling and the person being smiled at. Now that student didn't know all of that. He just knew that when he is smiled at he gets to feel like he's part of the human race, connected, acknowledged, and less than disgusting to a teacher who frowns every time she sees him. For all those reasons, it just makes him feel good.

A smile is the only facial expression that communicates to the animal brain - always concerned with survival—that it is safe. Only when the brain-body believes it is safe does it have the capacity to concern itself with anything else, whether that's learning, pro-social behavior, or anything else. Our neutral faces—you know the ones...our attempts to mask what we really feel inside—keep the brain-body on alert and in a greater state of alarm because of the need for the survival brain to err on the side of caution. Maybe our neutral face will end up shifting to a smile that will communicate greater safety, but maybe it won't. The recipient of our facial expression can't afford to wait to find out. He or she needs to be prepared for the worst because when prepared for the worst, survival is more likely. I understand why we try to hide our true feelings from the people we teach, work with, love, and care for, but I'm here to tell you (and there's no cartwheel happening here); it's a bad idea. It just doesn't work.

When my son was between three and four years of age, I was driving us around town on errands. When I tensed up slightly at the wheel because of something going on with traffic, he asked quickly and with alarm, "What's wrong, Mama?"

What do we usually say to people, especially children, when they ask us what's wrong? That's right.

We say, "Nothing." As we raise and teach children, however, we need to ask ourselves, *what exactly are we teaching them when we answer in this way?* Children at every age, from infancy all the way into young adulthood, are largely sensory beings that instantaneously pick up on EVERYTHING nonverbal, as though they are covered in billions of little sensory receptors. This is because the part of our brain most accessible to us at birth and throughout childhood is the primal, sensing, surviving part of our brain, the brain stem. Though we have the rest of the anatomy of the brain in place, the brain stem is the only part lit up, "online," activated, and "ready to go" at birth. The rest of our brain mass is quiet, dark, and inactive, in other words, inaccessible to us. (The only small exceptions to this are underdeveloped parts of the visual and auditory cortices. These are also lit up under an MRI because we can see and hear at birth but not as well as we will grow to with experience.)

These recent neuroscientific discoveries are how we now know that the brain is sculpted by experience. At birth, we have such a small and primitive part of the brain active. Every other part, with each of its sophisticated functions, develops *after* birth in response to the interactions we have with the environment. I don't know about you, but that answers the nature-nurture debate for me. It's *nurture, nurture, nurture,* and before you start telling yourself it's too late for that nurturing to happen now, I will remind you that it is never too late! The brain can learn and grow new neural pathways throughout the lifespan. If you'll recall from Chapter One, this is called neuroplasticity. As long as we are alive having experiences, our brain changes in response to those experiences, pruning the neural pathways associated with what we no longer engage in behaviorally, and building new neural pathways for what we *are* engaging in behaviorally. This happens whether we want it to or not, whether the behaviors we perform are healthy or unhealthy.

When we tell people nothing is wrong when something *is* wrong—especially children—we teach them to doubt what they *sense* is true. Their sensory radar is intact and they can see, hear, smell, feel, and sense when something is less than stress-free. This is a critical capacity that serves them well, and if we don't mess with it, it will continue to serve them well the rest of their lives. When we say, "Nothing," when there's *something*, no matter how slight, the children in our lives become confused and less secure about themselves *and* you. *What's the truth here? Who and what can I trust? My own experience? My own radar? You? Are you telling me the truth?*

Instead, with my own son while driving in the car, what I very fortunately knew in the moment to say was, "Wow! You can feel that, huh? Mama just got a little tense up here. I gripped the wheel, my shoulders went up...you saw that."

"Yes, mama. What's wrong?"

"Someone just cut me off up here and it made me a little nervous, but you know what? Traffic is clearing. I'm slowing down, and everything is going to be okay now. *I got you.*"

My goal through this exchange was to, of course, leave my son with a greater trust and security in himself, in his own capacity to use his senses to make judgments, knowing they are often accurate and certainly were in this case. These kinds of honest, fluid exchanges also serve to strengthen my credibility as a parent, and the bond I share with my son. As a result, we have a solid foundation for living together as honestly and healthily as possible.

The children in our lives need to feel a greater sense of ease in *our* nervous systems in order for their nervous systems to feel safe. That's just how it works. When they feel secure, they can concentrate on all the other things we want them to be able to do, like learn and socialize appropriately. If we are tight and tense and stressed and tired or miserable in any other way, whether we try to hide it or not, they know. I hate to tell you, but I must. *They know!* They can only do as well as we feel.

Let's hear that one again: The children in our lives can only do as well as we feel – and I don't mean once we've had our margarita. This is the tough part of my job. Parents want to drop their children off at my office, pay me to "fix" them, and then get on with their lives without having to make much change of their own. Business as usual doesn't work, not in the long run. It backfires in frightening ways. Their children, big and small, when dropped off to see me, begin to feel relief with 60 Seconds. They learn their tools and start using them. They end up feeling good, and this gives them hope that they'll be okay after all. But over time, as they continue to live with their parent(s) and it's business as usual, their wherewithal wears down, as it would with anyone. They feel duped that they had any hope at all, and they revert in ways that can be more frightening than before. It's so necessary for us as parents to practice what we preach.

Tim

Years ago, I had the privilege of working with Tim when he was 11 years old, four years after his mother suddenly died, leaving him terribly traumatized by the experience and loss. His father and only sibling participated in the therapy (his stepmother did not) and together we worked at all levels of the experience— thought, feeling, and sensation—in order to bring relief. I was careful to educate the father about what changes Tim was going through in his brain and nervous system and what expectations were going to be realistic for him until his amygdala calmed and he felt more safe and secure. The father learned how he needed to back off the more typical expectations of achievement for a time, and focus instead on nurturing their relationship and loving connection. If Tim's father and stepmother could make their relationship with Tim the focal point, if they could focus not on his grades and athletic performance but on his safety and security, on the quality of shared warmth and affection, Tim was going to be okay. Tim came around in many ways with this approach, and therapy paused.

Tim is 16 years old now, attending a private school and earning B's and C's. He catches himself having a hard time staying focused in class, often daydreaming, and struggling to get homework done. His dad and stepmom report that he complains often, wanting to blame his difficulties on the teachers, the environment, and them. Quite simply, Tim's not doing well because he doesn't feel good. He's supposed to be over his mother's death by now, right? The fact that he's not feeling good couldn't possibly be because his mother died when he was seven. That was a full nine years ago. His dad's over it: he's been married to someone new for almost seven years. His younger brother is over it too: his stepmom is the only mom he remembers. Tim feels alone in his feelings and wonders, like his family does, what's wrong with him. Why can't he just get on with life like they're getting on with life? Why can't he concentrate better and achieve more?

Tim explained that he has no memory of his life from the ages of seven to ten, and today he feels, as he has for a long time, "stuck." I explained that the "stuckness" he feels is inside his nervous system from the trauma of his mother's sudden death. His mother went to work one day and never came home. When he was *given the news, his brain did what it is designed to do. The amygdala sounded off its alarm and sent his body into a freeze. Remember, the survival brain has only three behavioral options: fight, flight, or freeze. When a seven-year-old unexpectedly learns that the person he is closest to and most dependent on is gone and never coming back, freeze is the choice of the brain—a numbing, dissociating, unfeeling, not-really-here-anymore response that protects the brain-body from all the pain associated with the loss. Hence, Tim remembers nothing from the three years that followed. He wasn't really in his body experiencing any of it. He has been floating, spacey, going through the motions, breathing but not noticing, walking on the ground, but not feeling it, not able to feel connected to anything or anyone, least of all himself.*

Now that Tim is 16, the expectation is that he'll keep up with homework, grades, sports, chores, and everything else. Dad understood through our work together five years ago that, Okay, it's going to take a while longer before we can really put any pressure on him for all of that. *But his stepmom, who did not come in and learn about the neuroscience and the importance of relationship and connection over achievement for a time, is thinking,* Okay now! Let's go! I want better grades. I want the homework done and the room picked up. I want you playing sports, and I don't want to hear the complaining.

Dad thought, Tim's got to get back into therapy. *However, the person who really needs "therapy" or 60 Seconds the most, is Tim's stepmom. Her levels of stress* and unresolved trauma have been gravely impacting Tim for a long time. Of course, it is often the case that the people who need help the most are the most resistant to it. Without the stepmom's willing participation the second time around either, I went ahead and met with Tim (and later his Dad) and I'm so glad I did. Revisiting 60 Seconds with Tim provided him a safe enough feeling in his body that he could notice, acknowledge, and connect with the stuck sensations without getting overwhelmed by them. As he sat in this balanced way with the scary stuck feeling, he became red in his cheeks with heat; he perspired, his hands and feet were tingling, and he yawned incessantly while his eyes watered—all outward signs of physiological changes on the inside. More specifically, these outward signs indicated discharge of the stress stuck in Tim's body from having been traumatized. Tim was experiencing an essential capacity of his own body to rid itself of the "stuckness." When I asked him what he noticed was happening inside, he very simply said with a look of surprise, "I feel good."

Tim's progress with discharging the effects of his loss doesn't mean he won't grieve. Of course, he will continue to remember his mom and feel sad sometimes, which I explained to him. He will experience the sadness differently, however, not in a way that feels stuck and scary, but in a way that feels more open and fluid. Though feelings of sadness, loss, and aloneness are difficult and uncomfortable, through the use of 60 Seconds, Tim will be able to notice the discomfort while feeling grounded and supported. This balance is what *keeps the feelings manageable and tolerable, allowing Tim to remain engaged in his life in a more present, joyful way.*

Tim has all the tools he needs to get to this good feeling place whenever he wants. However, because he lives at home with his family, if either his father or his stepmother continues to try "faking" it, Tim's future is at risk. More specifically, if his parents try to cover up their stress or unresolved trauma with lots of to-do lists, keeping everyone on the go achieving external goals instead of connecting with one another, or if they continue to check out in other ways, like with self-medication, Tim's hope may be lost.

When I met with Tim's Dad after my session with Tim, he let me know that he believes his wife needs to get help in order to learn how to give Tim more space or Tim "will throw himself off a bridge." We only need follow the stats on suicide in youth today to know how UN-farfetched this fear is. I educated the father about the importance of having his wife also learn 60 Seconds, either with me or with someone else who can work with her in a similarly physiological way. It remains to be seen whether or not this will happen.

Does this family have what it takes to get real about the dynamic at work, to accept that the effects of stress and trauma are taking a dangerous toll, and to trust me enough when I tell them it doesn't have to get worse before it gets better? I understand why this stepmother and so many others of us have been afraid to get help. The help we've gotten has many times not felt good at all. For some of us, it has made things worse. Whatever approach espouses digging things up, remembering what's in the past, or re-living painful memories as an essential part of the process may be losing support when it doesn't involve a physiological piece that soothes. Help is only "help" when it makes us feel good now, and that's exactly what 60 Seconds does. Let's feel good now, shall we? Here is 60 Seconds again:

1. Sitting in a chair, the couch, your car, or under a tree (it doesn't really matter where), uncross your legs or feet, and feel your feet flat on the ground.

2. Take in the support of what you are sitting in or lying in. Lean into the back of the chair, or feel your bottom sinking into the cushion of the couch.

3. Breathe in through your nose, simply noticing that you are breathing, and with each breath fill your belly with air. Breathe out through your nose or mouth, whichever feels most comfortable.

4. Visualize a soothing nature scene, such as the beach, a meadow or flowing stream, or imagine you are inside your container being protected.

5. *Most* importantly, notice what is happening inside your body as you utilize these tools:

grounding your feet; taking in *support*; *breathing* in through your nose filling your belly with air; and *visualizing* a safe, beautiful place.

- As you utilize the fifth tool, *noticing* what is happening inside, focus only on the *pleasant* physical sensations you are having. Consider some of the words that would describe these pleasant sensations: warm, flowing, calm, vibrating, tingling, spaciousness, openness, expansion, a reduction in tension or tightness, slowing down, getting heavy, getting clear, focused, stabilized, solid, balanced, or connected.

- If thoughts or unpleasant sensations enter into your awareness, simply go back to the beginning of 60 Seconds and do the steps again. Remember, the more you notice sensations, the less you will focus on negative or distracting thoughts.

Conclusion:
New Thought:
To Love You Is To Know You

A dear friend visited recently and told me he had just re-read *The Road Less Traveled* and was finding it very helpful. I thought, *Really?* That's the book that starts with, "Life is difficult." *Are we still there*, I wondered? Western culture as a whole may be, but I have to say, more and more individuals are ready for New Thought. We understand that what we focus on expands, that the stories we tell ourselves and the beliefs we hold have the power to make or break us. We decide whether or not life is difficult based upon the beliefs we hold – created by the thoughts we think, the stories we tell, the experiences we notice, and the feelings upon which we focus. This isn't just New Thought; this is new *science,* proven enough times now that we are paying attention.

My friend went on to say that yes, *The Road Less Traveled* was so helpful because it explained that people's problems are created by their avoidance of them. If they would just face their problems, they wouldn't get bigger and become so overwhelming. At least, this was the argument of the book, shared by my friend, and undoubtedly a logical and linear explanation that makes perfect sense. So why doesn't it have more traction in our lives? Why don't we face our problems more often than we avoid them? The answer is simple: because we want to feel good! And we haven't before been taught the tools to help us feel good when we are facing our problems.

Our behavior has long been ahead of the science that is now able to explain why we live for avoidance, delay, and denial. Aren't they awesome? I'm not being sarcastic. New Thought and the science that explains its effectiveness eliminate the negative connotations to these actions. They really do help. That's why we engage in them so often! They help us feel good. On an instinctual level, we know that we can only do well when we feel good.

Talk about useful tools! We have avoidance, delay, and denial down to an art form, and I dare say, why shouldn't we? We ALL want to get out of the rut we're in and be free of unhealthy habits. We ALL want to replace these habits with healthier alternatives because somehow we know if we do, we will feel more connected to who we really are. It sounds contradictory, doesn't it? We avoid, delay, and deny in an attempt to feel more connected to who we really are. What?! Yes, because who we really are is that person who feels at ease, patient, kind, loving, and connected to others without feeling threatened or needing to compete. When we avoid a problem we get temporary relief that helps us to feel more at ease, even if just for a moment. When we feel better, we feel more like our true selves and that's when we can connect with others in a way that feels authentic, meaningful, and alive. So why does all that feel too difficult to do on a regular basis without a margarita? Could it be because we *believe*, "Life is difficult?"

According to the neuroscience that supports New Thought, life doesn't have to be as difficult as it feels to us sometimes. For instance, we now know an essential ingredient we can add to our avoidance, delay, and denial tendencies to make them healthy in the long run. When we simply avoid, delay, or deny, without 60 Seconds, we get some immediate relief but don't usually end up feeling well later. Instead, we now know how to re-focus our attention so that we are both ignoring something that doesn't feel good *and* actively focusing on, and engaging in, the easier, healthier thing we can do that brings relief.

Let me give you my favorite example: my hiking buddy, Susan, goes hiking instead of cleaning the house, and I do mean, *all the time*. Okay, a lot of the time. (She's going to kill me.) And she's right too! (She'll like that part.) Doing something healthy that builds up in us a greater internal capacity to self-regulate actually gives us the neurochemical "juice" we need to ease our way into tackling a portion of the "problem." Here's the deal with hiking instead of doing 60 Seconds, however. Without the noticing piece of 60 Seconds—the conscious awareness of the sensory experience we are having from the activity – it takes a lot of hiking to finally get to cleaning the house. Doing 60 Seconds *while* hiking, however, makes neurons fire stronger and neural pathways for self-regulation deepen faster. The end result is the same, a calmer nervous system and a larger capacity to at least start on cleaning the house with greater ease. Yet, unlike the temporary fix we get from hiking, 60 Seconds *transforms* the nervous system. Its *sensory awareness* component gets us the quicker and longer-lasting result because it rewires the brain.

The simplicity at work here is this—ignore the problem and focus on the solution because **the solution is ALWAYS the same: get back to the good feeling state!** That's the state from which all great things happen. When we are in The Zone, we are internally balanced, neurochemically and in every other way. That balance is what gives us the capacity to clean the house. And more than that, it gives us creativity, passion, interest, curiosity, zest, flexible thinking, focus, and a greater capacity for all things "rad," like thinking outside the box and coming up with solutions where before there were none. **Quite simply, self-regulation heals, unites, solves, and evolves.**

Let's get there—into The Zone—conveniently, quickly, and in as many different settings as we can. Given the world's crazy pace, I'm talking about using tools on the go, with more than one or two on hand from which to choose: grounding, support, breathing, visualization, and noticing. Doing 60 Seconds over and over again in various ways, sitting, standing, lying down, hiking, shopping, driving, and waiting at the auto shop or hair salon, will give us what we need when we need it the most.

Let's talk for a moment about who we really are from a New Thought perspective. It is not what too many traditions or systems today would have us believe. Old Thought convinced many of us that we are flawed, disordered, or addicted in a way that requires long-term management through adherence to dogma, medication, or therapy. You may be noticing, however, that Old Thought is *keeping* some of us flawed, disordered, and addicted, as well as dependent on dogma, medication, and therapy. It isn't serving a growing number of us anymore because it doesn't get us closer to the good feeling state. It does the opposite. As we learned from The Chocolate Cake Study, sitting in our shame only leads us to cyclically engage in the same self-medicating behaviors that have hijacked our life. They bring us temporary relief at best. Practicing New Thought, with the help of 60 Seconds, allows us to be kinder and gentler with ourselves. It relieves the shame. Soon enough, we feel a greater acceptance of ourselves just the way we are. We may even find ourselves saying, "We is kind. We is smart. We is beautiful." (Hopefully, most of you saw the movie *The Help* and that was funny. ☺)

The truth is we are whole, capable, strong, alive, growing every day, learning all the time, and getting better and better, whether we're focusing on all that or not. Focus on all that, and watch what happens.

When we bring our attention to how far

we've come, when we take in the support always there in any given moment, and when we recognize the strengthening sensory experiences of 60 Seconds, we are well on our way to having the life we want. Just like the one group in The Chocolate Cake Study, we'll be savoring a little cake while slipping easily into our skinny jeans. Watch out! Now we've got self-regulation for moderation!

We may be noticing that calm, centered, grounded, and unreactive are becoming more permanent traits rather than temporary states. So-called problems feel smaller. It takes more to get upset. Upsets are less frequent, less extreme, shorter, with less damage to repair. The less overwhelmed we are inside our brain-body, the easier it is to do just about everything. 60 Seconds gives our brain-body a new, healthier focus without making us detached or disconnected—the side effects of self-medication.

One client of mine, a young adult named Barry, uses 60 Seconds "all day long," he told me, and said that the tool has significantly lowered his marijuana use. "I don't have to get messed up anymore, man! I'm so happy!" he said. "I've got a kid on the way. I don't want to be messed up anymore." As he smiled radiantly, he told me he has a "new problem. I don't know how to get this perma-smile off my face!" The palpable, massive, and infectious joy I experienced radiating from Barry that day was not from marijuana but from internal power. Barry was feeling his own capacity to self-regulate his emotions. His new discomfort with bubbling happiness was something I was not about to help him with, no matter how nicely he asked. ☺

Betty

When Betty, a middle-aged woman, came in to see me for the first time, she immediately shared that she had not been able to drive on the freeway for three years without having a panic attack. This was her presenting complaint and what she wanted to work on first. She also shared a long list of other ailments and disorders, such as asthma attacks, rebound anxiety, sinus infections, depression, and so on. She had been in and out of different treatment programs, trying various medications, therapies, and procedures over many years. Some had brought relief for a time but had not cured nor equipped her to sustain long-term results. Hearing from my other clients that they were healed by this approach allowed Betty to hope enough for one last try.

I guided Betty through 60 Seconds for approximately half an hour; the other half hour was spent discussing past treatment, current issues and hopes for a cure, as it seemed important to Betty that I understand where she was coming from. When she came to see me the following session, she was already driving on the freeway again with no feelings of panic at all.

Any time she felt the slightest provocation of stress, she used 60 Seconds to prevent the anxiety from increasing and easily continued driving.

By the third and last time I met with Betty, we simply celebrated that not only was she now getting off and on the freeway ramps all over town (each one had previously been a huge trigger of panic for her), but also she was driving over a large, looming bridge she had been avoiding for 30 years. When she drove over it the first time with no problem, she felt so liberated she turned around and immediately drove over it again! Talk about transformation.

Betty shared that she engaged in (and continues to engage in) 60 Seconds "religiously" since I first taught her the tool. She has also been doing it every day with her middle school special education students who are in sixth, seventh, and eighth grades. Now she says that she couldn't imagine teaching without it. Betty reported that 60 Seconds has been the "magic pill" she always hoped her anti-depressants would be. She described the effectiveness of the tool from the perspective of her background in physical education. The more often she engages in 60 Seconds, she said, the easier it becomes to use, much like muscles getting stronger the more they are exercised.

And then Betty's new thought bubbled up from her calmer physiology, echoing the many new thoughts of my clients over the years, which have always made me cry:

"I am enjoying my life."

Barry's new thought: "I can actually feel stoned without smoking my joint!"

Curtis' new thought: "It's only an hour and a half, it can't be that bad!"

Katlyn's new thought: "I know what peace is."

Debbie's new thought: "Nothing's wrong."

Other students and clients have said the following:

"One thing at a time. It'll get done."

"It doesn't have to happen this second."

"This isn't life-threatening."

"I'm okay right now."

"Everything's okay."

"I'm doing the best I can and that's enough."

"I'm enough."

Soothing the physiology of the body out of its activated state quiets the mind and replaces negative, scary thoughts of lack and urgency with more loving, compassionate thoughts of greater ease and peace. The more we get to the good feeling place through the use of 60 Seconds, the more automatically these new thoughts of ease and peace will be generated for all of us.

These neural pathways are here now, available to us, triggering a deep parasympathetic response because we've nurtured their growth. Life doesn't have to be so difficult. It just has to be conscious. And that's exactly what the tool does. It wakes us up! Colors seem brighter; food tastes better; orgasms are more pleasantly intense! I told you this was going to be good!

It's because 60 Seconds is an *experience*. We all know by now that reading a book about how to change is not enough to lead to change. (Though it can help! Thank you for reading. ☺) Our action plans, analyses, and insights may be great, but they don't make muster because they don't alter the brain. Remember, according to the neuroscience, only experience does. 60 Seconds is the most important *experience* to have because of how quickly it rewires the brain and nervous system for changes we want to make.

As we are nearing the end of this book, I want to stress that 60 Seconds is available to us anytime, anywhere. Life will always have hurdles and new challenges (how boring would it be otherwise?!) but after we learn 60 Seconds, stress won't have nearly the same overwhelming effect as before. Now that we are preparing to go out into the world with our new, bright, and shiny brain-body ☺, it may be helpful to recap some of the new things we've learned:

- **All adaptive, pro-social, healthy, achievement-oriented behaviors require self-regulation.** Self-regulation is the single most important foundational capacity for what we say we want—healthy, happy relationships at work and at home, greater focus, better concentration, an increased capacity to follow through on plans, as well as a greater ability to be consistent, reliable, dependable, less reactive, and more in control.

- If we want more peace and balance, we need to *experience* more peace and balance – *inside.*

- *Noticing* when we are having a stress response cues us to start self-soothing with our tools.

- When we are in constant stress mode, our amygdala convinces us we can't afford to take the time for anything or anyone, least of all 60 Seconds. Even if someone we love is right there in front of us needing our presence in that moment. "No," says our brain-body. "I don't have time for you! I have important things to do!"

- In fact, we can't afford NOT to do 60 Seconds. Any time a stress response happens, our toolkit can be used to restore calm and balance so we can stay in relationship with the people we love.

- Using the tools as often as possible, and with awareness, is what strengthens their capacity to work automatically.

- "Zero-ten-ing" is not good for our health, though it is what the brain-body *naturally* does when under extreme stress. We can do better now.

- Visualizing our protected, safe and powerful self within our container can help restore strength and calm. What are we trying to keep up with anyway? The image our parents have for us, somebody else's definition of success? Or maybe the image driving our excessive behavior is our own, based upon what everyone else seems to be doing; maybe we're trying to fit in, believing more money will bring greater happiness. Achievement feels good. I get it. But if it's not for our own definition of success and happiness, maybe we need to get anchored back in our container to connect again with what *we* really want.

- When we are in The Zone of optimum physiological arousal, with just enough anxiety to keep us interested, to engage our motivation and to focus our concentration, we do our best. When we are out of The Zone with too much or too little anxiety, we don't feel good and our performance is hindered.

- **60 Seconds won't stop us from chipping away at our to-do list; it actually helps us execute plans with more precision, greater calm, better focus, and bigger joy.** So, by all means, keep going, doing, and conquering – I'm not suggesting a drastic change in lifestyle. No matter our goals or values, on or off the treadmill of life, in or out of the "rat race," 60 Seconds offers a simpler way to transform our life into an experience that feels more balanced, peaceful, and grounded in purpose.

- **60 Seconds is a safe alternative to self-medication.** It's the cheapest drug *not* on the market. In fact, not a single one of the tools costs a penny.

- **The less we grab at that unhealthy fix, the weaker the neural pathways associated with that habit become.** Don't focus on the thing you wish you could stop. Don't even talk about it. Just do 60 Seconds and you will actively build neural pathways for the more peaceful, joyful state it brings.

- Worrying or talking about a problem without sensory relief causes stress to build and *that* wreaks havoc on the body, perpetuating discomfort rather than solving the problem.

- While doing 60 Seconds, whatever you are noticing or not noticing is perfectly okay. Focus on the tools that are working for you without concern for any that are not easily accessible in that moment.

- 60 Seconds can be used in a variety of ways—employing all five tools at once, which may be the most powerful way, or using whichever one or two of the tools we can, when we can. If all we can do while driving our car is notice our breathing, then we are still, as simple as it sounds, rewiring the brain on the go.

- Bonus (and my personal favorite ☺): When we are using 60 Seconds transparently, we light the way for our children to do the same.

Now that we have quick and easy tools that effectively get us feeling good in our body, we no longer need to escape from life, and *when we aren't escaping, we are connecting*—with our children, our loved ones, and ourselves.

With 60 Seconds—five little tools in one little minute—we are well on our way to "self-medicating" naturally and healing the nervous system permanently. No more escaping or coping through the moment, putting on a Bandaid, surrendering our power, or white-knuckling through. With 60 Seconds, we transcend the minutiae of our lives, the stress and pressure of it all, the old ways of surviving another day for another dollar. By giving our brain-body a whole new experience of being in the world without getting carried away by it, we experience the kind of joy that can only come from our own self-governance.

My title promises *"surprising"* joy for a reason. *It is surprising!* I never believed I could have the kind of peace I have in my own skin without beer! Are you kidding me? But I do! Not perfectly, not everyday – but there it is, again and again. Peace, and the exquisite joy that comes with it. And I know it's because 60 Seconds has rewired my nervous system. My upbringing prepared me to survive and do well. That was never the question. The shocker has been living a full, present life with meaningful connection to my family, friends, and work—rather than simply working hard, succeeding by some external measure, and checking out when needed.

Even though life is still busy (that hasn't changed!), I use 60 Seconds everyday—sneaking it into all the moments I'm doing something else—*and* I thank my son for reminding me on the days I need prompting! ☺ He knows as well as I do that the better I feel, the better I do.

Let's hear that one last time: *The better I feel, the better I do.* It's true for all of us. So let's just focus on feeling better! Let's protect and strengthen what we've been creating for ourselves that might be vulnerable to the chaos of everyday life. Even after you put this book down, remember that opportunities to use 60 Seconds are everywhere. You have all that it takes to become more aware of your inner state, no matter what level of stress you're experiencing. Ask yourself, *Am I in or out of The Zone?* That awareness alone, coupled with your toolkit, will give you a palpable experience of the power you have over yourself. And *that's* a fix!

Appendix
Top Ten Questions Most Frequently Asked By Parents

Parents want to know what's best for the brain development and self-regulatory capacity of their children. This rising level of consciousness is thrilling for me. I will address the most commonly asked questions here with a sound adherence to the effectiveness of 60 Seconds as the most powerful parenting tool I know (from firsthand experience, believe me).

1. *Is it ever okay to leave my baby crying in the crib until he or she finally falls asleep?*

Not if you want your child to develop a healthy capacity to self-regulate. If you leave your baby in the crib to cry to sleep, you begin the cycle of "zero-ten-ing." Excessive or prolonged crying, protesting, or "tantrum-ing" is the "ten." Passing out from exhaustion is the "zero." This early behavioral pattern sculpts the nervous system over time, creating greater automaticity of these responses. The "zero-ten-ing" pattern becomes habitual as its corresponding neural pathways become more deeply embedded in the brain. This can happen with just one single searing experience, or after any number of experiences. Each person's nervous system has its own unique level of sensitivity, which affects whether or not the pattern becomes habitual. Sensitivity is determined by genetics, environmental conditions in the womb and thereafter, and depends upon variables such as previous experience with stress or trauma and availability of resources. The "zero-ten-ing" pattern is challenging enough with our infants. It is not something we ever want at later stages of development. Preventing its progression from the beginning will be a gift that keeps on giving.

Excellent resources can help you get your child to sleep in healthy ways. I like Harvey Karp's books because his information and approach is brain-based. I also highly recommend a book called, *Secrets of the Baby Whisperer*, which gives the same important message I give: as you become more grounded in your self, more self-regulated, and therefore more in the present moment with awareness, you will be able to see what your baby needs and you will be able to respond in just the right way that will lead to greater health and well-being for both of you. Do your 60 Seconds, over and over again wherever you are and as often as you can. When you do, soon enough you will have created in your nervous system an automatic capacity to *pause*. Pause is necessary in order to observe your baby without feeling an uncontrollable urge to rush into the situation with only a reactive guess as to what will soothe the situation. Knee-jerk reactions are rarely helpful. Rather, a sensory-based response is often called for.

Toddlers and children can be guided through 60 Seconds while trying to fall asleep if they are having difficulty. This has worked beautifully with my son. Simply guide your child as he or she lies in bed to bend his or her knees up so feet are flat on the mattress. I like to put one of my hands on Jules' feet and the other on his chest as I remind him to breathe deeply in through his nose (out through his nose or mouth, whichever is easier to do). Then I guide him to notice the support of the bed beneath him and to let the bed do all the work of holding him, allowing him to sink into it. I ask him to notice how soft the pillow is under his head, how comfortable the sheets and duvet cover are. I rarely get to this point without him yawning like a roaring lion and turning to his side to give in to his parasympathetic putting him to sleep.

2. My toddler really struggles with temper tantrums and other difficult behaviors. Can some kind of therapist help?

I am not a fan of "pathologizing" anything. In other words, I do not like to identify anything as a problem that needs to get fixed. And I don't like our children getting the message that something is wrong with them that they now have to go get help for from a stranger. My own therapist was instrumental in solidifying this as my opinion. Because my son was born with a rare blood disease and has been subjected to several stressful and traumatic experiences as an infant and toddler, I thought when he became aggressive for a time in pre-school that sending him to my therapist for somatic healing would be a great thing. My wise therapist told me that it was me who needed a tune-up to deepen my own self-regulation, as it had been shaken up by going through my son's illness with him. After *my* tune-up, everything with my son "magically" got better...go figure. ☺

We have to start with us. This is always true. When we are more regulated, less reactive, more grounded, and less fearful, our children feel safer and do better, no matter what is going on in their life. They will always benefit from us getting healthier. Start with you.

So, as they are having that tantrum, please do not talk at that time, and do not abandon either. Stay close enough, with some healthy distance if you need it to stay calm. Do your 60 Seconds. Your words will trigger a larger reaction from your child, and will prolong the length of time the tantrum persists for all the neuroscientific reasons I discuss in my publications and videos. Please refresh yourself of this information if you have forgotten the reasons why we ALWAYS need to be using fewer words and going sensory no matter what stage our children are in, infancy, childhood, adolescence, or *adulthood.*

When your child's tantrum is over, and during times of little to no stress, focus on practicing 60 Seconds with your child, or other grounding sensory tools you may have or know. Of course, I am partial to 60 Seconds, not because I created it, but because it is INTERNAL to us. The internal balance of self-regulation frees us from needing anything external to soothe, like sitting on a fit ball, pushing hands into the wall, or running hands under hot water, all of which are also helpful. Only when the nervous system is calm, remind your children of who they *really* are, always giving the message that you know they would do better if they could. We have to be the ones that *know* our children *want* to do it a different and better way, and *they do, when they can.*

We need to remember, highlight, and focus on all the successes. Tantrums and other difficult behaviors are NOT something our children choose to engage in. Such behaviors are an indication that our children's higher capacity to reason has been hijacked by their more primitive brain due to some perceived threat that may or may not be real. The solution or intervention always involves practicing soothing sensory tools, especially 60 Seconds, to rewire the brain and nervous system for greater tolerance and less reactivity.

Some other helpful ways to "go sensory" include spending more time in nature, with animals, moving, balancing, playing, cuddling, singing, and taking family classes like cooking, painting, crafts, yoga, or meditation. Lighten it all up; quiet it all down; spend more time together having fun without media or technology.

3. Is it ever okay to spank my child or use some other form of punishment?

There is no neuroscientific support for the use of punishment. It simply doesn't work. Please review The Chocolate Cake Study to remember that the shame elicited by punishment is the same shame that comes from us bringing attention and reflection to times when we made a bad choice and suffered the consequences. The bad feeling state leads to more "bad" behaviors. As The Chocolate Cake Study teaches us, it is much more effective to focus on successes and sit in the good feelings that come from remembering those. Then we have all the good "juices" pumping through our bloodstream, allowing for better choices with greater ease. Consequences with compassion is the way I like to go, and one of my favorite consequences is to require that whatever damage is caused by the upset, whether physical or emotional, gets repaired. Not by forcing an apology but by having them take an action that "rights the wrong" as much as possible—a good deed, for example. It serves the nervous system well to get the better feelings that come from taking an active part in repair. Our children feel safe, understood, and loved when we help them do that. When they feel safe, understood, and loved, they are better able to make a healthier choice next time.

4. My doctor (or husband or mother) wants me to stop letting my child have his or her pacifier. What should I do?

Educate them about the fact that our babies and toddlers do not possess their own internal soothing mechanism, the parasympathetic branch of the autonomic nervous system, until they are three years of age. They need things external to them until that age to help regulate their arousal. If they are older than three and still want the pacifier, you can be certain they are feeling an inordinate amount of stress in *their* particular brain-body so please do not take the pacifier away without replacing it with something else that serves the same soothing function—something healthy, such as their "blankie" or soothing music. NOT something technological, like having television on as background noise or sitting them in front of the television or videogames. My recommendation will always be 60 Seconds as the replacement, because of how quickly and deeply it works at developing self-regulation, and because it is internal to the person. Nature, animals, sleep, hydration, something healthy to eat, a fun interactive game to play, laughter, movement, are also excellent to engage in when wanting to soothe stress and at any other time.

Some younger children (and plenty of older people as well) may not be able to sit to do 60 Seconds, and that's fine. *Standing* and feeling their feet on the ground imagining roots growing out from the bottom of their feet, letting their arms be branches stretching up into the sky and flowing in the breeze, breathing air into their belly as though blowing it up like a balloon—younger children respond to this approach very well.

Don't be surprised to know that untold numbers of M.D.s and Ph.D.s do not know the current neuroscience and are continuing to practice within an old paradigm that simply does not work for growing numbers of children (and parents). I encountered one such pediatrician for my own son who wanted the pacifier out before Jules was three because it was ruining his teeth. I did not follow the M.D.s terrible advice—so bad I can't even repeat it here—and Jules' teeth are just fine, as is his capacity to self-regulate in spite of the multiple traumatic experiences he's had.

5. Should I send my child to pre-school or keep him or her home another year?

That depends upon the level of stress at home. If you, as the parent, are able to self-regulate your own emotions well, and have an attuned relationship with your child, having your child at home with a balance of experiences could be a beautiful thing. I do not believe in rushing childhood in any way whatsoever. However, if you are overwhelmed or have not established your own healthy capacity to self-regulate your anxiety, it would be healthier for your child to get to experience the nervous systems of others, especially after you have taken the time to find a good place from visits and interviews. You don't need to feel guilty for this! In fact, parenting from a guilty place is one of the biggest culprits of problems in our culture today. When you are aware and honest and realistic about the amount of care you can provide in a healthy way, you're making a great decision for your child that you should feel good about. As you begin to use 60 Seconds for your own healing while he or she is in school, you will be able to spend more time together because you are both able to be in the good feeling place. We want the times you come together to be in good health.

6. Should I send my child to a special kind of pre-school, such as a more play-based program, or are academically focused pre-schools okay?

Children need far more play, willful handwork like knitting, physical movement, and experiences in nature than they are currently getting in academically focused programs. I am a firm believer in play-based pre-schools (and kindergarten programs) for many sound reasons that come from neuroscience and other scientific sources. For example, we know from one important study cited in David Elkind's article on the importance of play to brain development and later achievement, that at the end of a pre-school year, the children who attended a play-based pre-school did just as well on the same academic benchmark as children who attended an academically focused program.[15] The alarming and unacceptable difference between the two groups of children was that those who attended the academically oriented program had higher levels of blood pressure, heart rate, and cortisol. While the brain and nervous system are at such an exquisitely sensitive time of development, it will never be my recommendation for any child, no matter how smart or capable or seemingly ready, to attend an academically focused program over a healthy play-based one. Every child deserves a prolonged period of childhood play, which ironically lays all the necessary groundwork for academics anyway. Remember, pre-school is just the beginning of a long educational career. Our children's capacity to finish the marathon of education with success depends upon their capacity to self-regulate in the earliest years of school. Excessive cortisol from early academics does not help to this end.

7. What are the dangers of our children spending time on technological gadgets, playing videogames, and the like?

Technology has a specific effect on the nervous system. We know that each time a little "bling" sounds off on our cell phone, for example, a surge of endorphins gets released in the brain-body that keeps us going back for more. Many self-identified excessive videogame players explain that it is "addictive" to earn points on videogames and get higher and higher scores when it all happens so quickly. Instant gratification is what we get from all the bells and whistles. And as we know, it doesn't work that way in life. The danger with spending too much time on technology—and too much time varies for each individual—is better understood when we take a look at how the brain develops: in a use-dependent fashion. That means our brain develops the capacity to do what it repeatedly experiences and does not develop neural pathways for what it does not experience. If the brain's experiencing repeated, instant gratification, that's all it knows how to do. It doesn't have neural pathways for delaying gratification, in other words, for persisting at a task even when the payoff doesn't come until later.

The excitement elicited by the bells and whistles of videogames and texting can't be matched by anything in life. Everything else becomes boring in comparison. Our teaching, for example: how do we top that dog and pony show? We are responding to the call for more technology in education now, which I am not against as long as we balance out our use of technology in schools with experiences of nature and social interaction. What we *cannot* do is cut out all the healthy ways we trigger the parasympathetic branch of the nervous system – the experiences that give us a more open, expanded, flexible feeling of ourselves, and replace them with a narrower focus on a screen, and therefore, a more regular stress response.

Technology, such as searching the web or playing a videogame, is a narrow experience that requires tunnel vision—a focus on what's right in front of us. This is a small, tight place that leaves our brain-body feeling tense and sore over time. Nature, by contrast, allows us to orient to the world around us and opens and expands our nervous system by triggering a soothing parasympathetic response. Technology causes a sympathetic response, as you'll notice. Our heart rate goes up, as does our blood pressure, when we are checking our emails, texts, Facebook messages, LinkedIn invitations, tweets, and winks on Match.com. Managing all of the technology we do does not help us feel more relaxed in the long run. While engaged in these activities, if we were hooked up to a machine that measures physiology, the findings would be undeniable.

Time spent on technology is time not spent in nature and interacting interpersonally. Again, we only develop neural pathways for the experiences we engage in. Right now, we are getting better at being isolated indoors and moving our thumbs, and getting worse at being with each other or noticing how nature balances it all out. Over time, have we not noticed which feels better? Are we so disconnected that we are no longer aware which experience feels healthier? This is precisely why I am so passionate about 60 Seconds. It helps us to connect again, to ourselves, to nature, and to others in a way that allows us to notice what's true and what's not, what feels healthy and what feels like a distraction, or a way of numbing, escaping, and disappearing. Though the escaping feels adaptive for a time, 60 Seconds will help us not need to cope or adapt in such a way, at least not as often. Rather, 60 Seconds helps us to be here now, authentically ourselves, able to connect and feel and thrive.

8. Isn't homework necessary to increasing achievement and ensuring responsibility?

No. I am against homework in the elementary years of education for reasons soundly based in science. There is a plethora of research that can be found from multiple sources including www.stopthehomework.org. [16] Homework in the elementary years does NOT now, nor has it ever, increased achievement. In fact, it has the opposite effect because of the stress it causes and the time it robs from children to play and rest and be silly, all necessary to the development of self-regulation. Family stress because of homework has the potential to destroy fundamental family time and enjoyment of one another at the end of an already hectic school and workday. Teacher morale may also be at risk due to the stress of assigning, collecting, grading, and discussing with parents and students homework issues. The way a school day is structured now, with more time spent on academics, and less time spent balancing that out with the arts, nature, and physical exercise, children are SPENT at the end of the day, as parents are! Throw homework on top of that and don't be surprised by the increases in anxiety and apathy my audiences report from across North America.

In the middle school years, up to one hour, all subjects included, raises achievement, and up to two hours in high school, ALL subjects included, raises achievement. However, anything above this amount of time spent on homework begins to decrease achievement due to the burnout in the brain-body that is created by doing too much, much like athletes cannot practice more than two hours and 15 minutes or their performance in the game is impeded by exhaustion.

Teachers, please simply grade children on what they do for you in class. If you want your students to learn a greater sense of responsibility, send them home with a rock and tell them to bring it back the next day. Parents, please chill on this issue. Putting too much pressure creates the opposite result you're seeking. Third grade burnout is a real and growing phenomenon, as is high school dropout. It's time to connect the dots between our insistence on too much, too soon, too fast and the results we now face, including an increase in childhood suicide in boys and girls as young as eight. Enough is enough.

I am not against reading at home in the evening or any hands-on projects that bring lessons to life when they are not too stressful for children to get done within a reasonable amount of time, especially when they involve nature! However, if you are going to insist on homework other than reading and fun projects, you MUST allow your child to come home and regulate FIRST with a fun, healthy activity for as long as he or she needs in order to get into The Zone you now know about. Once our children are regulated and in The Zone, homework is far more of a breeze. Otherwise, as you have experienced, it can take children hours upon hours to do their homework because of their level of exhaustion directly after a school day. Using 60 Seconds for greater relief, ease, and self-regulation must come *first* in order to set the foundation for comfortable academic performance later. Pain for gain does not work when it comes to brain development. The brain-body does not excel this way. It shuts down.

9. *What about team sports and other ways we may be overscheduling our children? Is it ever a good thing to do?*

The word "overscheduling" here reveals that for the inquiring parent(s), it feels like too much. We have a gut feeling that we need more down time, all of us, and in general, we have a gut feeling of the answer before we even ask professionals for their advice. I wish we would all rely less on professionals and become better at hearing and listening to our own sense of what feels good and right for our own family. When we become more present and connected through the use of 60 Seconds and other sensory tools that help us get out of our analyzing-ad-nauseum head, we'll come up with our own answers that truly are the healthiest thing for our children and for us.

I caution here, however, about team sports before the age of eight, and again, I recommend looking up David Elkind's work to understand more about why this is. Before the age of eight, our children's level of cognition is such that criticism about how to hold the bat, and how to run, and how to hit harder and better and stronger, and get the technique down just so, whether we want to call this criticism "constructive" or not, is too much for the *developing* brain-body to tolerate. It increases unhealthy stress in children under the age of eight to be told over and over again how they're not getting it quite right and how they need to be doing it differently than what at this juncture in their development is coming naturally to them.

It's like when we send kindergartners home from school with sad faces on their less than perfect spelling tests. We do some well-intentioned analyzing with them, stating that, *The "frowny" face isn't because you're bad. It's your behavior that's bad. See the difference? It's not you. It's your behavior we don't like.* And they look at us with their barely developing cognition without a clue of what we're talking about. Their level of cognitive understanding tells them that when they don't get it "right," they're "wrong." That's just how it is. *If I'm not right, I'm wrong. If I'm wrong, I'm bad. If I did something bad, I am bad.* The bad feeling state depletes our children (as it does us) of all the essential biochemicals they need to do well.

Even when it seems our children are enjoying playing on a team, when there are numerous rules of conduct and performance, eventually the fun fizzles. Our young children don't realize the toll this takes on their brain-body over time, just as we haven't. We have learned through our research on play[17] that when we start with all of this too soon, stress accumulates and leads to shutting down, giving up, and quitting prematurely. Team sports are great after age eight. Before age eight, however, children need lots of unstructured, spontaneous play where there is no right or wrong, just their imagination.

10. How do I help my child cope with all the pressure these days to achieve more and faster and better, in every area of their life, socially, academically, and beyond?

Many of us are fighting the good fight, trying to educate the people in our life and our children's life about New Thought explained by current neuroscience and it feels like an uphill battle. People look at us like we are crazy when we try to eliminate, or at least reduce, homework or we ask for greater consciousness through more mindful meditative practices in schools. I know how resistant or skeptical people can be. But please, do not stop the conversation. Do not stop educating with the science and spreading the word that there is a more balanced solution to what may feel like endless pressure. 60 Seconds and other sensory tools such as yoga, mindfulness, and other types of meditation help us transcend to a better way of being. **Please model 60 Seconds transparently for your children. Let them see you getting healthier, stronger, and less reactive as you practice the tools more and more often. Then, they will be more open to learning how to use 60**

Seconds for themselves. The tool, comprised of five individually powerful tools, as you know, is exactly what will help them tolerate and transcend the social and academic pressures of life. And they love it, by the way! 60 Seconds is being used with great success in pre-K-12 schools all over North America. Data collection shows a consistent 20-70% decrease in stress with corresponding increase in calm and focus.[18] Here is what children of all ages are reporting:

"When I do the 60 Seconds, all my problems go out of my head. I don't think about them anymore."

"When I do 60 Seconds, I feel like I can do anything."

"When I do 60 Seconds, the test doesn't scare me anymore. I feel more relaxed."

"When I do 60 Seconds, my grades go up!"

"When I do 60 Seconds, I feel calm and strong and powerful."

Teachers report that their students remind them to do the 60 Seconds when the daily ritual slips through the cracks during hectic days. In fact, several teachers shared that when they were away from their classes, the students taught the substitute teachers how to do 60 Seconds so they wouldn't miss their chance to do it! Teachers tell me their students "absolutely love the tool! And so do I! This is helping ME!"

I'll leave you with one last story that comes from my work with another young person who I believe is leading the way for all of us to get healthier:

Teddy

Teddy is a 14-year-old boy attending an alternative high school for students who, due to behavioral challenges (the inability to self-regulate), are no longer able to go to regular school. Teddy came darting into the office area one day holding his shoulder, swinging his arm, and pacing back and forth frantically stating, "I need an icy-hot! I need an icy-hot! My shoulder! It's killing me!"

Because the staff present at that moment knew of my 60 Seconds, they thought it an excellent opportunity to see me, and the tool, in action.

"Teddy," the psychologist said, "There is someone here who could work with your shoulder in a different way than with the icy-hot. Would you be willing to give it a try?"

"What is it?" he asked.

I jumped in and explained that it's something hard to describe but more easily understood when experienced. "Let's just give it a go and see what happens. Okay?"

"Okay."

"All I want you to do right now is exactly what you're doing because it's giving you some relief. Notice how good it feels to at least be moving around this room, holding your shoulder, and swinging your arm." I knew NOT to try to get him to sit down. That would have been in resistance to what was offering his brain-body some

relief at the moment. What I needed to do was replace his need for soothing in this particular way because it was only minimally effective, and, not to mention, it was disruptive to the school. I needed to replace his current coping with something even more soothing that would actually allow for the healing of the injury, as opposed to putting a bandage on it.

"Teddy, I want you to feel your feet stomping on the ground. Can you feel how your feet are making contact with the ground and how solid that floor is beneath you? Notice that as you move about the room. Focus on your feet."

"Yeah. I feel it," he said as his pace naturally began to slow down. Without prompting, he made his way to the wall. He leaned into it, stood still, held his shoulder, and no longer paced or swung his arm. As he leaned against the wall, I mirrored him and stood leaning against the wall as well.

"I want you to take in the support of that wall now, Teddy. Feel your back leaning into it, feel its support. Notice that?"

"Yup."

"Okay, so your feet are solidly planted on the ground. You've got all your weight on your feet. Notice that. And you're getting support for your back from the wall. Notice. (Pause.) Now add something else for me. Breathe in through your nose. Can you do that?"

"Yup."

"Okay. (Pause.) Now I want you to imagine some place you want to be that feels good, like a warm beach or a lush green mountain top."

"Hey, I do this when I try to fall asleep at night," he said. "I go to the beach."

"Can you see the beach right now?"

"Yup, I can see the beach. I can hear the waves. I do this at night."

"Okay, so now I want you to be at the beach in your mind's eye while you're feeling your feet on the ground and the support of the wall. (Pause.) *Teddy, check back in with your shoulder. How's the pain now?*"

Perfectly calmly, Teddy said, "It's gone."

"It's gone," I said. "And about how long did that take, would you say?"

He shrugged his shoulder and said, "A minute."

I got goose bumps in that moment—of course because the tool is called 60 Seconds! I had already started writing this book and knew in the moment Teddy spoke those words I wanted him in it. I wanted Teddy to be in the book for all the kids out there who want to calm down and feel better. They want to focus and pay attention. They want to relax and "get it together." The only reason they aren't calm and feeling better, relaxed and staying focused, paying attention and "getting it together," is because no one has ever taught them how. *So can we wake up now, and hear the good news, learn the new science, and listen to the children in our lives asking for exactly what they need? You know the first thing Teddy said as soon as he started enjoying the relief he was experiencing from five little tools in one little minute? He immediately asked: "Hey, can we teach this to my mom?"*

About The Author

Clinical and school psychologist, Dr. Regalena 'Reggie' Melrose, is the creator of *Brain Charge: The K-12 Curriculum* and the author of the ground-breaking books, *You Can Heal Your Child* (Bush Street Press, 2009) and *Why Students Underachieve* (Rowman & Littlefield, 2006). She is a sought-after international speaker and consultant specializing in the application of current neuroscience to educational practice and parenting. Dr. Melrose maintains a successful private practice in Long Beach, California, as a stress and trauma-healing specialist for children, adolescents, and adults.

References

1   Maté , G. (2012, September 30). Dr. Gabor Maté on ADHD, Bullying and the Destruction of American Childhood. YouTube video retrieved from http://www.youtube.com/watch?v=UrZL2CnUSRg

2   Mukherjee, S. (2012, April 19). Post-Prozac Nation. *The New York Times*. Retrieved from http://www.nytimes.com/2012/04/22/magazine/the-science-and-history-of-treating-depression.html

3   Ljótsson, B., Andréewitch, S., Hedman, E., Rück, C., Andersson, G., & Lindefors, N. (2010). Exposure and mindfulness based therapy for irritable bowel syndrome–an open pilot study. *Journal of Behavior Therapy and Experimental Psychiatry, 41*(3), 185-190.

4   Zeidan, F., Johnson, S. K., Diamond, B. J., David, Z., & Goolkasian, P. (2010). Mindfulness meditation improves cognition: Evidence of brief mental training. *Consciousness and Cognition, 19*(2), 597-605.

5   Davidson, R. & Tippett, K. (Host). (2012, June 14). Investigating healthy minds. *On Being*. Podcast retrieved from

http://www.onbeing.org/program/investigating-healthy-minds-richard-davidson/transcript/4715

6   Davidson, R. J., Kabat-Zinn, J., Schumacher, J., Rosenkranz, M., Muller, D., Santorelli, S. F., & Sheridan, J. F. (2003). Alterations in brain and immune function produced by mindfulness meditation. *Psychosomatic Medicine, 65*(4), 564-570.

7   Hölzel, B. K., Carmody, J., Vangel, M., Congleton, C., Yerramsetti, S. M., Gard, T., & Lazar, S. W. (2011). Mindfulness practice leads to increases in regional brain gray matter density. *Psychiatry Research: Neuroimaging, 191*(1), 36-43.

8   1 Corinthians 4:20, New King James Version.

9   MacInnis, D. (2011, July 10). Human behavior: To resist temptation, forget guilt or shame and think positive. *Los Angeles Times*. Retrieved from http://articles.latimes.com/2011/jul/10/opinion/l a-oe-macinnis-selfcontrol-20110710

10 James, W. (1890). *Principles of Psychology.* Harvard University Press.

11 Wissel, H. (1994). Shooting: A state of mind. *Scholastic Coach*.

12 Lindamood, P., Bell, N., & Lindamood, P. (1997). Sensory-cognitive factors in the controversy over

reading instruction. *Journal of Developmental and Learning Disorders, 1,* 143-182.

13 Gendlin, E. T. (1981). Focusing. New York: Bantam Books.

14 Frisch, T. (2012, August). What ails us. *The Sun, 440.* Retrieved from http://thesunmagazine.org/issues/440/what_ails_us

15 Elkind, D. (2008). Can we play? *Greater Good Magazine, 4.4,* 1-3.

16 Bennet, S. (2009). Stop homework. Retrieved from http://www.stophomework.com

17 Elkind, D. (2008). Can we play? *Greater Good Magazine, 4.4,* 1-3.

18 Melrose, R. (2013, January 31). K-12 curriculum *Brain Charge* is now evidence-based! Retrieved from http://drmelrose.com/2013/01/31/k-12-curriculum-brain-charge-is-now-evidence-based/

Resources

Websites

The Foundation for Human Enrichment – www.traumahealing.com

Edutopia - What Works in Education – www.edutopia.org

Rick Hanson - Resources for Happiness, Love & Wisdom – www.rickhanson.net

Healing Resources – www.healingresources.info

Sensorimotor Psychotherapy Institute – www.sensorimotorpsychotherapy.org

The Alert Program – www.alertprogram.com

Canadian Foundation for Trauma Research and Education – www.cftre.com

Race To Nowhere – www.racetonowhere.com

Stop The Homework – www.stophomework.com

Electronic App for Healthy Living – www.getsomeheadspace.com

Dr. Regalena "Reggie" Melrose – www.drmelrose.com

Books

Elkind, D. (2006). The power of play: How spontaneous, imaginative activities lead to happier, healthier children. New York, NY: De Capo Lifelong Books.

Gendlin, E. T. (1981). Focusing. New York, NY: Bantam Books.

Halbert, B. L. (2013). Embracing defiance: Helping your child express their unique voice while keeping your sanity. San Francisco, CA: DB Publishing.

Hanson, R. (2009). Buddha's brain: The practical neuroscience of happiness, love, and wisdom. Oakland, CA: New Harbinger Publications.

Hogg, T. (2005). Secrets of the Baby Whisperer: How to calm, connect, and communicate with your baby. New York, NY: Ballantine Books.

Karp, H. (2000). The happiest baby on the block: The new way to calm crying and help your Newborn Baby Sleep Longer. New York, NY: Bantam Books.

Karp, H. (2004). The happiest toddler on the block. New York, NY: Bantam Dell.

Levine, P. A. (1997). Waking the tiger: Healing trauma. Berkeley, CA: North Atlantic Books.

Levine, P. A. (2010). In an unspoken voice: How the body releases trauma and restores goodness. Berkeley, CA: North Atlantic Books.

Levine, P. A. & Kline, M. (2006). Trauma through a child's eyes: Awakening the ordinary miracle of healing. Berkeley, CA: North Atlantic Books.

Levine, P. A. & Kline, M. (2008). Trauma-proofing your kids: A parents' guide for instilling confidence, joy and resilience. Berkeley, CA: North Atlantic Books.

Louv, R. (2008). Last child in the woods: Saving our children from nature-deficit disorder. Chapel Hill, NC: Algonquin Books.

Melrose, R. (2006). Why students underachieve: What educators and parents can do about it. Lanham, MD: Rowman & Littlefield.

Melrose, R. (2009). Hope and healing activities book: An activities book for adults working with school-aged children. Long Beach, CA: 60 Seconds Press.

Melrose, R. (2009). Hope and healing: A guide for parents of traumatized children. Long Beach, CA: 60 Seconds Press.

Melrose, R. (2009). You can heal your child: A guide for parents of misdiagnosed, stressed, traumatized, and otherwise misunderstood children. Long Beach, CA: 60 Seconds Press.

Melrose, R. (2012). Brain charge: Sensory awareness for student achievement. Long Beach, CA: 60 Seconds Press.

Siegel, D. J. & Bryson, T. P. (2011). The whole brain child: 12 revolutionary strategies to nurture your child's developing mind, survive everyday parenting struggles, and help your family thrive. New York, NY: Delacorte Press.

Magazines

Mindful Magazine, Taking Time For What Matters – http://www.mindful.org

Audio

Levine, P. A. (1999). Healing trauma: Restoring the wisdom of your body. Louisville, CO: Sounds True.

Levine, P. A. (2001). It won't hurt forever: Guiding your child through trauma. Louisville, CO: Sounds True.

Levine, P. A. (2007). Sexual healing: Transforming the sacred wound. Louisville, CO: Sounds True.

Melrose, R. (2006). Why students underachieve: What educators and parents can do about it. Available from http://www.drmelrose.com.

Made in the USA
Columbia, SC
22 September 2022

67291262R00119